Contents

Licence

Text © 2008 Barbara Mottershead (Eat more fruit and vegetables), Sandie Kendall (Puppets; Playgrounds), Nerys Tudor Jones (Moving pictures), Lancashire County Council, represented by Adrienne Dawes (Wheels in motion)
© 2008 Scholastic Ltd

Published by Scholastic Ltd, Villiers House, Clarendon Avenue, Leamington Spa, Warwickshire CV32 5PR

Printed by Bell & Bain Ltd, Glasgow

123456789   8901234567

British Library Cataloguing-in-Publication Data
A catalogue record for this book is available from the British Library.

ISBN 978-1407-10028-9

Visit our website at www.scholastic.co.uk

CD developed in association with
Footmark Media Ltd

Authors
Barbara Mottershead,
Sandie Kendall, Nerys Tudor Jones,
Adrienne Dawes

Series Editors
Louise T Davies, Sandie Kendall

Development Editor
Kate Pedlar

Editors
Kim Vernon, Fabia Lewis

Series Designer
Joy Monkhouse

Designers
Melissa Leeke, Andrea Lewis,
Shelley Best

Cover photographs
© 2007, JupiterImages Corporation

Acknowledgements

With thanks to: The Design and Technology Association for reference to helpsheets; British Nutrition Foundation for use of material from their website, Food – a fact of life.

Every effort has been made to trace copyright holders and the publishers apologise for any omissions.

© Crown copyright and other Crown copyright material. Reproduced under the terms of the Click Use Licence

Due to the nature of the web, the publisher cannot guarantee the content or links of any of the websites referred to. It is the responsibility of the reader to assess the suitability of websites.

The rights of Barbara Mottershead, Sandie Kendall, Nerys Tudor Jones and Lancashire County Council (represented by Adrienne Dawes) to be identified as the authors of this work have been asserted by them in accordance with the Copyright, Designs and Patents Act 1988.

Minimum Specifications:
PC: Windows 98 SE or higher
Processor: Pentium 2 (or equivalent) 400 MHz
RAM: 128 Mb
CD-ROM drive: 48x (52x preferred)

MAC: OSX preferred
Processor: G3 400 MHz
RAM: 128 Mb
CD-ROM drive: 48x (52x preferred)

List of resources on the CD-ROM

The page numbers refer to the teacher's notes provided in this book.

INTRODUCTION

This book and CD-ROM support the teaching and learning of a selection of units from the QCA Scheme of Work for design and technology at Key Stage 1. Some of the more successful and popular units from the QCA scheme have been kept while fresh themes and ideas have been developed for teachers who would like to move their scheme of work forward; units now include links to ICT. The full range of skills and knowledge across the design and technology subject area are covered within the five chapters included here (food, textiles, structures and systems) with a clear progression of skills in all areas through each of the three books in this series.

The activities in every chapter lead the teacher through all the necessary elements of a design and technology project, ensuring that it is well structured, comprising of a design and making assignment, focused practical tasks to develop skills and investigative activities to evaluate existing products. In each chapter children are encouraged to focus on the user and purpose as well as the function and aesthetics, creating a final product that fulfils specific criteria that they themselves set at the beginning of the project. In addition, children are introduced to designing strategies that will lead them to more creative and innovative ideas for their projects. Additional support and resources (such as ideas for investigations, video clips or step-by-step guidance on how to make items) have been provided for those QCA units that have been seen as difficult or more technical to teach.

Resources on the CD-ROM
All the images, sound and video clips on the CD-ROM have been specifically chosen to support the teaching of these units and broaden the areas of study. They include photographs, for example of different types of bag, photograph frames and salad ingredients, and film clips showing ways to cut fruit and vegetables, how to sew using a variety of stitches and different types of lever in action.

Photocopiable pages
The worksheets in the book accompany the children's investigations, focused practical tasks and design and make activities. They can be used to build a process diary for each unit, which should be supplemented with any other sketches, photographs and written work the children create as part of the project.

Word cards and glossaries
The vocabulary of design and technology is often new to the children and therefore there are word cards and glossaries provided on the CD-ROM where necessary. These can be used as worksheets to be read through with the children or the cards can be used to label display materials.

Health and safety
Notes on health and safety are provided in the introduction to each unit, and photocopiable sheets are provided on the CD-ROM illustrating safe usage of equipment, such as hand drills and hacksaws. Always use any advice in this book and CD-ROM in conjunction with your own school policy.

Contexts
Outcomes in design and technology are usually more successful when the children understand why they are undertaking a particular project. They need to be clear about the problem or need, the person or people affected by this need and the resources available to realise solutions to that need. Although some suggestions for final products are made, such as making a night light for a child's bedroom in 'Lighting it up', these should be considered carefully when setting the task: the context will influence the direction that the children's ideas take.

HOW TO USE THE CD-ROM

Windows NT® users

If you use Windows NT® you may see the following error message: 'The procedure entry point Process32First could not be located in the dynamic link library KERNEL32.dll'. Click on **OK** and the CD-ROM will autorun with no further problems.

Windows Vista™ users

If you use Windows Vista you may see the following error message: Click on **OK** and the CD-ROM will autorun automatically.

Resources on this CD-ROM can be viewed using an interactive whiteboard, data projector or PC.

Setting up your computer for optimal use

On opening, the CD-ROM will alert you if changes are needed in order to operate the CD-ROM at its optimal use.

To see images at their maximum screen size, your screen display needs to be set to 800 x 600 pixels. In order to adjust your screen you will need to **Quit** the program.

If using a PC, open the **Control Panel**. Select **Display** and then **Settings**. Adjust the **Desktop Area** to 800 x 600 pixels. Click on **OK** and then restart the program.

If using a Mac, select **Displays** under **System Preferences** and choose 800 x 600 screen size from the list of options.

To print PDF versions of the images and to view and print the photocopiable pages you need Adobe® Acrobat® Reader® installed on your computer. This can be downloaded from www.acrobatdownload-ib.com.

To view the videos you need QuickTime™ installed on your computer. This can be downloaded from www.apple.com/quicktime/download.

Menu screen

▶ Click on the **Resource Gallery** of your choice to review the resources available under that theme.

▶ Click on **Complete Resource Gallery** to view all the images, videos and audio files available on the CD-ROM.

▶ Click on **Photocopiable Resources** to view and print the photocopiable resources also provided in the book that accompanies this CD-ROM.

▶ Click **Back** to return to the opening screen.

▶ Click **Quit** to exit the program.

Resource Galleries

▶ Click **Help** to find support on accessing and using images.

▶ Click **Back** to return to the **Menu**.

▶ Click **Quit** to exit the program.

Viewing images

Small versions of each image are shown in the Resource Galleries. Click and drag the slide bar to scroll through the images in the gallery, or click on the arrows to move the images frame by frame.

▶ Click on an image to view the screen-size version of it.

▶ To return to the gallery click **Back to Resource Gallery**.

Viewing videos

Click on the video icon of your choice in the Resource Gallery. In order to view the videos on this CD-ROM you will need to have QuickTime™ installed on your computer (see 'Setting up your computer for optimal use' above).

Once at the video screen, use the buttons on the bottom of the video screen to operate the video. The slide bar can be used for fast forward and rewind. To return to the Resource Gallery click on **Back to Resource Gallery**.

If you encounter any problems when viewing footage, check that your computer fulfils the minimum specifications (see page 2). If there are still problems running the footage, try using a different version of QuickTime™ (such as 7.13.1).

Printing

Click on the image to view it (see 'Viewing images above'). There are two print options.

Print using Acrobat enables you to print a large copy of the image as a PDF file. These are often a higher quality than printing images from the screen. Once you have printed the resource, minimise or close the Adobe screen using – or X in the top right-hand corner of the screen. To return to the Resource Gallery, click on **Back to Resource Gallery**.

Simple print enables you to print the image without the need to use **Adobe® Acrobat® Reader®**. Select the image and click on the **Simple print** option. After printing, click on **Back to Resource Gallery**.

Slideshow presentation

If you would like to present a number of resources without having to return to the Resource Gallery, you can create a slideshow.

In the gallery, click on the + tabs at the top of each image you would like to use. It is important that you click on the images in order; a number will appear on each tab to confirm the order. If you would like to change the order, click on **Clear slideshow** and start again.

Once you have selected your images – up to a maximum of 20 – click on **Play slideshow**.

To move between slides on your slideshow, click on the blue arrows either side of the screen.

You can end your slideshow presentation at any time by clicking on **Back to Resource Gallery**. Your slideshow selection will remain selected until you **Clear slideshow** or return to the **Menu screen**.

Photocopiable resources

To view or print a photocopiable resource page, click on the required title on the list and the page will open as a read-only page in **Adobe® Acrobat®**. In order to access these files you will need **Adobe® Acrobat® Reader®** installed on your computer.

To print the selected resource, select **File** and then **Print**. Once you have printed the resource, minimise or close the Adobe screen. This will take you back to the list of PDF files. To return to the **Menu**, click on **Back**.

Using this CD-ROM with other programs

To switch between this CD-ROM and other programs on your computer, hold down the 'alt' key on your keyboard and then press 'tab'.

Technical support

For all technical support queries, please phone Scholastic Customer Services on 0845 603 9091.

EAT MORE FRUIT AND VEGETABLES

Content and skills

This chapter links to Unit 1C 'Eat more fruit and vegetables' of the QCA Scheme of Work for design and technology at Key Stage 1. The chapter encourages children to be aware of the variety and diversity of foods available. Photographs and videos are available on the CD-ROM to demonstrate the foods available and the techniques required.

Through a range of focused practical tasks, children will develop an awareness of the variety of different fruit and vegetables available. Through investigation and practical work, they will gain an understanding of a range of different ingredients, equipment and making skills that can be used, as well as increasing their sensory vocabulary. They will find ideas for making new products through investigation and practical work and will gain an understanding of healthy eating through looking at the eatwell plate.

The chapter is structured as follows:

▶ Investigating and evaluating fruit and vegetables.
▶ Making a dip.
▶ Making dippers.
▶ Practise making dips and dippers.
▶ It's cool to compare.
▶ Shopping around.
▶ Design and make activity.
▶ Evaluating their dips and dippers.

Outcome

The main outcome of this chapter will be for children to design and make a dip and some dippers for an event or person of their own choice. In doing this, children will be expected to:

Photograph © 2007, Peter Rowe

▶ gain an understanding of the properties of a range of fruit and vegetables, including taste, texture and appearance
▶ gain an understanding of the eatwell plate
▶ investigate and evaluate a range of dips and dippers
▶ make decisions about what product they are going to make based on their investigations and evaluations
▶ prepare and combine ingredients into a specific product
▶ use basic tools safely
▶ recognise that it is important to eat more fruit and vegetables.

Health and safety

When working with food it is important to demonstrate accurate, effective and appropriate use of equipment, using safe and hygienic working practices. Ensure that:
▶ surfaces are cleaned down with antibacterial cleaner
▶ a plastic table cover is kept for food activities and used to cover wood/old tables
▶ aprons are provided for food preparation
▶ there are appropriate storage facilities
▶ food equipment is kept in a clearly labelled cupboard
▶ safe practice is taught in relation to using equipment such as knives – refer to your school's health and safety policy.

Remember to obtain parental permission before tasting sessions to identify any cultural or dietary restrictions. Children who are unable to eat certain types of foods due to allergies should be offered alternatives.

Links to other subjects

Science: finding out about a balanced diet; skills such as describing, sorting, sequencing; talking about food crops.

Maths: counting fruits and vegetables; ordering – smallest/largest; estimating how many pieces; adding pieces of fruits and vegetables together to make a total; taking pieces away and saying how many are left; finding totals – *how much does one apple and one orange cost altogether?*; measuring – *does the apple weigh more than the banana?*

English: word-level work such as, reading labels; naming equipment; words to describe characteristics of foods and parts of foods; sentence-level work such as, writing captions to accompany a display; text-level work such as, reading poems about food; writing a simple recount of the design and make activity.

Geography: identifying countries where different foods and dips originated.

ICT: data handling, for example, making a chart showing favourite fruits; using a digital camera to record food processing skills learned through focused practical tasks.

Organising the unit

All three types of activity should be undertaken (investigating and evaluating, focused practical task, design and make). The order in which the are undertaken can be of the teacher's choosing. For example, starting points could be:

▶ setting the design and make activity
▶ investigating the kind of dips of which the children are already aware
▶ a discussion of healthy and unhealthy food.

Resources on the CD-ROM

The gallery of resources on the CD-ROM includes photographs of collections of fruits and vegetables, to help the children to recognise the different ingredients that could be included in the products they make. Also pictured are photographs of a range of different dips that are available and ingredients that could be used as dippers. The 'Eatwell plate' is included as a photograph, showing the standard way of teaching about food groups. Fruit, vegetables and dairy foods are focused upon in particular.

Photograph © 2007, Peter Rowe

There are further supporting resources for teaching practical skills. These include video clips of food preparation skills – cutting and peeling.

Photocopiable pages

Photocopiable worksheets in the book and on the CD-ROM include:

▶ sensory descriptors to use when describing fruit, vegetables, salad ingredients and dairy foods
▶ a sheet showing a large variety of food items for children to cut and paste onto a blank version of the eatwell plate
▶ a recipe for making a tomato salsa dip
▶ a planning sheet for the design and make activity
▶ a worksheet for evaluating dips and dippers.

INVESTIGATING AND EVALUATING IDEAS

EAT MORE FRUIT AND VEGETABLES

Photographs: Fruit, Vegetables, Dipper foods, Dips, The eatwell plate

Photocopiable pages: Looking and tasting, The eatwell plate, Images of foods   **PAGES 14–16**

The photographs in the gallery of resources, on the CD-ROM, are used throughout the chapter in the investigating activities, focused practical tasks and evaluation activities.

The photographs provide an opportunity to show the children a variety of ingredients that could be used to make different dips, and also the fruits, vegetables and other ingredients that could be used as dippers. There are photographs of many kinds of fruits and vegetables, all of which could be used in focused practical tasks and the design and make activity.

Photographs of different kinds of dips and dippers are included to raise the children's awareness. The dips originate from all over the world and this point can be highlighted.

Discussing the photographs

▶ Look at each of the relevant photographs from the CD-ROM, and ask the children if they are able to name the different ingredients – view the 'Fruit' and 'Vegetables' photographs in the first instance. Have they eaten any of the ingredients? If so, have they eaten any them at home, and how often?

▶ Discuss with the children some of the foods in the photographs, asking questions such as: *Do you know what this is? Who has eaten one like it?*

▶ Discuss with the children what they understand by dips and dippers and show the photographs 'Dipper foods' and 'Dips'. Ask them what they think dips and dippers are. Have they tried any? How many types of dips and dippers can they think of? When do they think these dips and dippers are eaten?

▶ Show the 'Dips' photograph and discuss where some of the dips originate from, for example, raita (India), guacamole (Mexico), tzatziki (Greece). When do they think these dips might be eaten in that country? Ask the children to find the countries on a world map.

Activities

▶ Choose a number of sample ingredients from two food groups – fruit and vegetables and milk and dairy foods, to display for the children. Try to choose foods that are in season as these will be less expensive. In addition, include one or two more unusual foods that the children may not come across before but would find exciting to look at. Discuss simple ways in which the foods could be sorted, for example, colour and shape and feel.

▶ Children can start collections of pictures of fruit and vegetables, similar to foods on the classroom display, and paste them into their books.

▶ Encourage the children to taste small pieces of the samples. Begin by tasting a food that the children will be familiar with, to build their confidence. Describe the appearance and ask questions such as: *What do you think the inside of this looks like? What colour do you think it will be? What words can we use to describe its colour and shape?* Model how the children should taste the samples and perhaps record their comments, for example: 'This yogurt smells of strawberries. When I put it in my mouth it is soft, creamy, sweet and has small pieces of strawberry in it. It is easy to eat.' This is an opportunity to develop descriptive vocabulary with the children.

▶ Some samples will need preparing and this should be done in front of the children. Explain that a handful of the vegetables or fruit is roughly one portion, and that they should try to eat at least five portions of fruit and vegetables each day. The 'Looking and tasting' photocopiable on page 14 can be used for this activity. The children could work in pairs or small groups to investigate an ingredient and then explain to the rest of the class two or three things they have learned about that ingredient.

▶ Link the investigation to specific people or characters in storybooks to help the children to use their imaginations, for example, ask which vegetables they think Charlie and Lola would like to eat and why.

▶ Arrange a visit to a market, allotment or farm to look at vegetables and/or fruit that are

growing. Take photographs to display in the classroom on your return. Ask the children questions relating to where each of the foods come from.

▶ If fruit and vegetables are they grown in the school garden they could be harvested by the children. Carrot tops and pineapple tops could also be grown in the classroom.

▶ Show the children some shop-bought dips and dippers and discuss on what occasions they might be eaten – a snack, a party, a picnic?

▶ Allow the children to taste some dips and experiment with different dippers. Dips could be raita, salsa, hummus, taramasalata. For dippers, try vegetable sticks, pitta bread, unsalted pretzels and crackers. Help the children develop a sensory vocabulary while tasting these, remind them to notice appearance, smell, taste and texture.

▶ Discuss with the children what different ingredients the dips contain. Can they guess what might be in the dips? Show children the raw ingredients for various dips. Explain that dips are often made with a main base ingredient with other ingredients and flavourings added, for example, the base might be cream, cheese, yogurt, fruit or tomato. Record your findings as a group writing the name of the dip in the middle of the board and around it the different ingredients it contains (or make this part of a display).

▶ Ask the children what dippers are. (Dippers are ingredients used to scoop up the dip; these are often fruit, vegetables, bread or crackers.)

▶ Teach the children that foods can be sorted into five groups. Show the children the 'Eatwell plate' photograph and other images from the gallery, and use the ingredients from one of the dips as a demonstration. Help the children to identify which groups the dip (and dipper) ingredients belong.

▶ Repeat this with other dips and dippers. The children could practise sorting ingredients into the different food groups. This is an opportunity to talk with the children about the need to eat a variety of foods from the different food groups in order to stay healthy. Ask the children to use the 'Eatwell plate' and 'Images of food' photocopiables, on pages 15 and 16, to make a picture of their own balanced meal. (The children can cut out the illustrations of food on page 16 and then sort and stick them into the correct groups on their own copies of the eatwell plate.)

FOCUSED PRACTICAL TASKS

MAKING A DIP

Photograph: Dips
Videos: Cutting: (bridge technique), Cutting: (claw technique), Peeling

Photocopiable page: How to make a tomato salsa   PAGE 17

This activity allows the children to observe a dip being made and to think carefully about how one is constructed and how it can be changed. Use the videos to demonstrate the cutting techniques. Demonstrate mixing, stirring and combining techniques.

Decide which dips to demonstrate to the children so that they understand how a dip is made. The 'How to make a tomato salsa' photocopiable on page 17 shows the recipe, equipment and method. You may want to show the 'Dips' photograph from the CD-ROM.

Discussion

▶ Discuss the ingredients that, if added, would make the dip a different colour or texture, for example, a basic hummus could be changed by adding chopped red peppers, or a cheese and chive dip could have sesame seeds sprinkled over the top.

▶ Discuss how the dip could be presented, for example, it could be layered, marbled or presented as a shape. Ask the children how could they could achieve these effects.

Activity

▶ Demonstrate how to make a dip. Use the tomato salsa recipe on page 17 or choose one of your own. Start with one ingredient, for example tomato, yogurt, or a fruit, and then add others to it. As the ingredients are being prepared, show the children how they should work safely with equipment. Use the videos or demonstrate yourself how to peel and cut

ingredients safely and how to create different effects, for example, cucumber can be sliced or cut into chunks. Allow some of the children to join in, if appropriate.

MAKING DIPPERS

Photograph: Dipper foods
Videos: Cutting: (bridge technique), Cutting: (claw technique), Peeling

This task allows the children to witness dippers being prepared. Have available a number of ingredients with which to make dippers. Display the 'Dipper foods' photograph from the CD-ROM which shows a suitable group of ingredients. Some ingredients may be bought to use as they are, such as blinis, unsalted pretzels, bread sticks. Some may need a little preparation such as slices of pitta bread or tortilla. Others will need preparing, for example celery sticks, broccoli florets, carrot sticks, cucumber sticks.

Discussion

▶ Discuss what the ingredients are. Ask the children if they have tasted any of them before. Where do they think they are grown, and what are they made from? Ask them which ingredients they think could be used as dippers, without any preparation; which ones will just need a little preparation and which ones will need to be peeled, and cut up quite a lot.

Activities

▶ Show the children how to work safely and hygienically and encourage some of them to help as you prepare your work surfaces and collect the equipment together.
▶ Demonstrate how to prepare the dippers appropriately, using the cutting and peeling techniques shown in the videos on the CD-ROM.

PRACTISE MAKING DIPS AND DIPPERS

This activity allows the children to have a go at making dips and dippers themselves. Have a list of appropriate dips prepared, which the children can choose from. Try to ensure that a variety of different dips and dippers are produced throughout the class.

Discussion

▶ Discuss the dips and dippers you have demonstrated in the last two focused practical tasks. What did the children think of them? Go over the various techniques used in preparation and make sure that the children are all comfortable with these. Discuss what dips the children might like to prepare.

Activity

▶ Let the children practise some of the skills demonstrated and produce different dips and dippers. Remind them of the health and safety considerations listed at the beginning of the chapter. This activity will give them the opportunity to practise using equipment safely.

IT'S COOL TO COMPARE

This activity gives the children the opportunity to evaluate the different dips produced in the last activity and compare them to the shop-bought varieties.

Discussion

▶ Discuss how the children might compare the samples. Ask them what kinds of words they might use, what kind of criteria they would have. Talk about how they might comment on how a dip looks and then on how it tastes. Model the descriptive process for them, for example, 'This cheese fondue is a light yellow colour and looks creamy. When I put it in my mouth it is warm, smooth, creamy and tastes of cheese.' As well as descriptive words, you could ask the children to evaluate the dips by using 'smiley faces'.
▶ I really like this…
▶ This is okay…
▶ I don't really like this…

Activities

▶ Compare the dips made in class with the shop-bought varieties. Alternatively, try comparing different varieties of cream cheese, for example. Can the children tell the difference between the samples? Which one do they prefer? Which one do they think looks nicer? Can they use some of the descriptive and sensory words they have learned to describe what each dip looks and tastes like? Encourage the children initially to describe the appearance of the dip and then describe the taste and feel.

▶ The children could compare the dips using statements such as, 'I prefer this (homemade) dip to the other one because it is smoother, a brighter colour or, this (homemade) dip is not as good as the other because it tastes too much of tomatoes.'

SHOPPING AROUND

Here, the children have the opportunity to visit a market, shop or supermarket and to look more closely at where you can buy the items for dips and dippers.

Discussion

▶ Before the trip, discuss what the children will be looking for and what they will be doing. This could include:
  ▶ identifying the different foods from a sheet prepared beforehand
  ▶ drawing the ingredients and labelling the different parts
  ▶ describing the foods – the colours, shapes and sizes
  ▶ listing which ingredients would be used in a dip and which could be used as dippers.
  Remind the children that this is an opportunity to think about ingredients they could add to their own dips.

Activity

▶ Visit a market, shop or supermarket so that the children can look closely at vegetables, fruits and dairy foods before they have been bought and made into dips and dippers. They should conduct the activities you have agreed on during your discussions.

DESIGN AND MAKE ACTIVITY

DESIGN AND MAKE A DIP AND DIPPERS

Photograph: The eatwell plate
Photocopiable page: Planning my dip and dippers   PAGE 18

Explain to the children that they are now going to use all the knowledge and understanding from the preceding activities to design and make a dip and some dippers for an event or a person of their own choice. The children could work individually, in pairs or in groups to produce the dip and the dippers.

You may decide that the design and make activity would be best carried out over two or three sessions. The children could design and plan in the first session, which would enable the chosen ingredients to be available for the second session. The second session could be for making, and the final session for evaluating.

Give the children the following design brief: 'You are going to make a dip and some dippers for an event or a person of your own choice.'

Discussion

▶ Before starting the activity, discuss the purpose of the dips and help the children to develop their criteria for the type of dip they want to produce. Discuss the sort of dips and dippers they might make. Identify for what or whom the dip and the dippers will be made. *Will it be for a snack, a picnic, a party, a cultural event?*

▶ Remind them of the dips and dippers they have tasted and those they have already made. What ingredients did they include and what ingredients could be added? *How important was it that the products looked attractive and that people should want to eat them?*

▶ Remind the children that they should be using foods from the fruit and vegetables and dairy foods sections of the eatwell plate.

Activities

▶ The children should begin to think about the dips and the accompanying dippers they want to make. Try the following activities to help them to develop some ideas:

▶ Choose a base for the dip – for example, tomato, cream cheese or hummus. Add two or three ingredients to it. Draw and label the ideas.

▶ Take an existing ingredient, for example, cottage cheese and think of as many chopped vegetables as possible that they could add to it.

▶ Make a list of flavourings down one side of a page and a list of bases for the dips down the other. Draw lines connecting them in to pairs. Ask the children which ideas they think will work? *Are any of them good ideas? Which are the best ideas?* You may want to limit the children to three or four ingredients for their own dips.

Photograph © 2007, Peter Rowe

▶ Plan a dip with the children as a demonstration. Talk through all the considerations – the ingredients, equipment and method they will use.

▶ Look at the 'Eatwell plate' photograph with the children to identify which food groups are represented in the demonstration dip and dipper.

▶ Help the children to plan what they will be making and guide them to think about the ingredients, equipment and method they will use. Ask them to complete page 'Planning my dip and dippers' photocopiable on page 18 to help with this.

▶ Help the children to get organised for making their dips, and allow them time to complete their work. Ensure that they follow the necessary hygiene and safety steps. Encourage them to follow the plan they made. If they are working in groups or pairs encourage them to work together effectively, for example one child could carry out an action such as peeling and the other could check that this is being done safely.

EVALUATION

Photocopiable page: Evaluation PAGE 19

It is important to allow the children to evaluate their own product and the dips and dippers made by their peers.

Discussion

▶ Display all the dip and dippers that the class has made. Discuss the similarities and differences between the dips. Ask the children how the dips look different. *How do they taste different?*

▶ Ask the children to talk about their work to the rest of the class. What did they do? How did they do it? How would they do things differently if they were to make the dips and dippers again? Ask them if the dip and dippers meet the original purpose – for the identified person and/or event. *Could the dips and dippers be used?*

Activities

▶ Ask the children to use the 'Evaluation' photocopiable on page 19, to evaluate the finished product against the original criteria. They should also consider presentation and taste.

▶ The children should then taste and evaluate each other's dips and dippers. Ensure that they evaluate all the products fairly – in the same way. They should be encouraged to offer positive and helpful comments.

Looking and tasting

▶ Describe the food.

▶ Use the wordbank to help you.

Name and drawing of food	What does it look like?	What does it feel like?	What does it taste like?

crunchy	crisp	sticky	skin	sweet	oval
					bumpy
hard	juicy	soft		creamy	pips

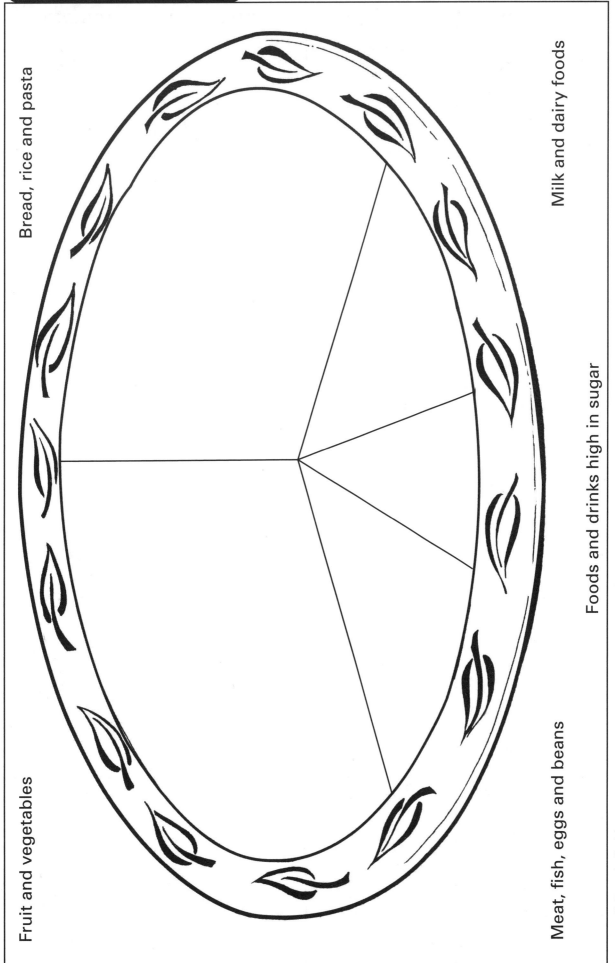

Bread, rice and pasta

Milk and dairy foods

Foods and drinks high in sugar

Fruit and vegetables

Meat, fish, eggs and beans

Images of foods

Carrots	Pineapple	Apple	Tomato
Cheese	Celery	Yogurt	Chickpeas
Avocado	Pitta bread	Cucumber	Onion
Crackers	Red pepper	Lemon	Pretzels
Bread sticks	Prawns	Tortillas	Poppadoms

Illustration © Beverly Curl

How to make a tomato salsa

Equipment

vegetable knife

measuring spoons

lemon squeezer

chopping board

measuring jug

pair of scissors

bowl for serving

Ingredients

5 tomatoes (about 500g)

2 tablespoons (30ml) olive oil

1 small red onion, finely chopped

100g cucumber, diced

1 tablespoon (15ml) lemon juice

4 basil leaves

a pinch of caster sugar

a pinch of salt

a little fresh ground black pepper

Method

1. Collect all the equipment.

2. Collect all the ingredients.

3. Wash the tomatoes. Chop into small chunks. Put into the bowl.

4. Slice the onion into small pieces. Put into the bowl.

5. Peel and finely chop the red onion. Add to the bowl.

6. Dice the cucumber. Add to the bowl.

7. Wash the scissors. Cut the basil into small pieces. Add to the bowl.

8. In the measuring jug mix together the lemon juice and olive oil. Pour over the other ingredients.

9. Add the salt, pepper and caster sugar.

10. Stir all the ingredients together. Cover and leave for about 30 minutes before serving.

▶ Describe how the tomato salsa:

Looks: _____

Smells: _____

Tastes: _____

Feels: _____

Planning my dip and dippers

▶ I am going to make a dip and some dippers for:

_____

The ingredients in my dip will be:

_____

_____

_____

My dippers will be:

_____

_____

My dip will taste:

_____

_____

My dip will look:

```
┌─────────────────────────────────────────────┐
│                                               │
│                                               │
│                                               │
│                                               │
└─────────────────────────────────────────────┘
```

This is how I will make the dip:

_____

_____

_____

This is how I will prepare the dippers:

_____

_____

_____

Evaluation

My dip looked _____

_____

My dippers looked _____

_____

My dip tasted _____

_____

My dippers went well with the dip because _____

_____

_____

Here is a drawing (or photograph) of my dip and my dippers:

The best thing about making the dip and the dippers was _____

_____

_____

I could have made things even better if _____

_____

PUPPETS

Content and skills

This chapter links to Unit 2B 'Puppets' of the QCA Scheme of Work for design and technology at Key Stage 1. This chapter focuses on using textiles to create puppets for a performance and on how different puppets are suitable for different styles of performance. The chapter also looks at the purpose for making a puppet and discusses who the user of the puppet will be.

The chapter encourages the children to investigate a range of puppets, talk about who would use them, and why and where they might be used. The children are encouraged to think about the purpose of puppets and whether all puppets are suitable for everyone, for example, could an adult or a child fit their hand in a glove puppet and would they both use it in the same way?

In the focused practical tasks, the children will have opportunities to learn about simple joining techniques for textiles, using a template or pattern to get the right shape and size for their puppet. They will learn how to decorate fabric using different methods to add colour and components, such as buttons or sequins.

The children will be taken through a design and make activity, which will include tasks that develop specific skills for working with textiles. They will be challenged to design and make a puppet to use in a performance or to help tell a story in a chosen venue.

The chapter is structured as follows:
▶ Investigating and evaluating puppets.
▶ Designing and communicating ideas.
▶ Making paper patterns.
▶ Creating the criteria for making.
▶ Simple sewing.
▶ Design and make activity
▶ Evaluating their puppets.

Outcome

The main outcome of this chapter will be to design and make a puppet that represents a character in a story, and to perform in the classroom (reading or role-play areas) or during an assembly. In doing this the children will be expected to:
▶ investigate a range of different puppets to see which is suitable for the intended performance
▶ discuss their ideas as they develop
▶ be able to say what their design has to do
▶ join two pieces of fabric together by stitching
▶ add features using appropriate materials and techniques
▶ create a puppet that works (that is, is the right size and reflects the character it represents and the purpose it is intended for).

Health and safety

When working with sewing equipment, the appropriate use should be demonstrated such as, storing pins and needles safely (for example, in a cork, to avoid injuries) and carrying scissors safely. The risk of injury is reduced if furniture is arranged appropriately and there is adequate lighting for pupils to carry out fine, close work.

The school and local authority health and safety policies and guidelines should always be referred to.

Photograph © Laura Neal / iStockphoto.com

Links to other subjects

English: The activities provide opportunities for the children to use skills such as, questioning; describing; speaking and listening. For example, children comparing two puppets will need to be able to observe and identify similarities and differences in the characteristics and talk about where would be suitable to use each puppet. The children can pose their own questions to investigate and evaluate puppets. This activity will also link with the children writing their own simple plays. Stories can be enacted by the children in a puppet show, further developing their speaking and listening skills.

Organising the unit

All elements of the unit should be covered but the order in which they are covered can be of the teacher's choosing. For example, starting points could be:

▶ the focused practical task that covers joining textiles together
▶ a visit to a museum
▶ the video clip of a puppet show

This chapter provides an opportunity for the children to work in groups in order to create all the characters from the story they are going to enact. The size of group will be dependent on the story that the children are going to tell. It would be advisable to use short stories with up to five characters, so that they can be easily adapted to small groups of children who at certain points in the activity will work together to make decisions.

Resources on the CD-ROM

The gallery of resources on the CD-ROM contains photographs showing a range of puppets (including those from different cultures) and different construction methods. These images are intended to supplement a class collection. They can be looked at, discussed (with different users and places for use in mind) and evaluated accordingly. The photographs of fabrics will help children understand that different types have different properties.

There is a video of a 'Punch and Judy' show and a puppet show from a different culture which can be compared and contrasted. A video to support the teaching of sewing techniques is also provided to help with practical tasks.

Photocopiable pages

Photocopiable worksheets in the book and on the CD-ROM include:

▶ worksheets to help the children investigate and evaluate a selection of puppets
▶ planning and design sheets that can be added together to produce a simple process diary for children to record their design ideas (these can be adapted for different contexts)

There are also photocopiable pages on the CD-ROM only including: 'Word cards: puppets', 'Template for a finger puppet', 'Template for a glove puppet'. Support sheets with advice on safe use of tools such as, scissors, are also provided.

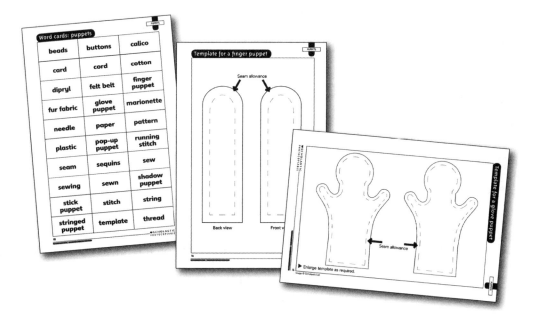

INVESTIGATING AND EVALUATING IDEAS

PUPPETS

Photographs: Finger puppets, Glove puppet – old man, Glove puppets – crocodile and zebra, Glove puppets – girl and wizard, Indonesian puppet, Pop-up puppets, Sock puppet, Stick puppet, String puppet, Dypril, Felt, Fur
Videos: Punch and Judy, String puppet

Photocopiable pages: Word cards: puppets (CD-ROM only), Investigating puppets, Evaluating puppets, **PAGES 27–28**

It is important that the children are able to explore and evaluate a variety of puppets. The children can bring in puppets from home to add to the collection in school. The photographs and videos in the Resource Gallery can be used to begin the evaluation activities. You can complete the evaluation process with the whole class or in smaller groups.

Encourage the children to identify the materials used, who might use the puppet, and where. It is through these activities that the children can identify what they will need to include in their ideas for a puppet. This knowledge and understanding will help them to decide on the appropriate criteria that they will use to generate, develop and make their ideas become a reality.

Discussing the photographs

▶ Use the photographs to demonstrate the types of puppets that are available – those for small-scale performances in the reading or role-play area (such as a finger puppet) and those for larger-scale performances in the hall during assemblies (such as a large hand or string puppet). Ask questions that lead the children to analyse which features need to be changed for different purposes. Ask them about the size of the puppet and whether it will fit everyone's hands.

▶ Show the photographs of different types of fabric: 'Dypril', 'Felt' and 'Fur' and ask the children which they recognise. Discuss the properties of the fabrics. *How do they feel? How strong are they?*

▶ Look again at the photographs of the puppets and discuss the materials used in the puppets' construction. Ask the children to identify materials that have been used to make the different parts of the puppets such as, the body and eyes. Discuss why wood is used for the parts that the user holds for example in the stick puppet (they need to be rigid) while soft fabric is used for other puppets such as, glove puppets (they need to move with the hand.)

Discussing the videos

▶ Watch the video 'Punch and Judy' and discuss how well the puppets are used to tell the story or show feelings, during the puppet show.

▶ Discuss the differences between the string puppet and Punch and Judy: how they move; where the user is (above or below); colours and fabrics; which the children prefer and why.

Activities

▶ Use the sheet 'Word cards: puppets' from the CD-ROM to familiarise the children with the main vocabulary associated with the topic.

▶ Ask the children to identify their favourite puppet and explain why they like it. Ask them to identify any materials and components used in the construction of the puppet. They can record their thoughts on the 'Investigating puppets' photocopiable on page 27.

▶ To help the children understand that the choice of puppet is dependent on where they are going to use it, take them to

Photograph © Lisa Gagne / iStockphoto.com

areas in the school where the performances may take place, for example, the hall, the drama space or studio, another classroom, or the library. Ask them to identify which puppets would be suitable for use in the areas visited. Encourage the children to record their ideas on the 'Evaluating puppets' photocopiable on page 28.

FOCUSED PRACTICAL TASKS

DESIGN AND COMMUNICATION

Photocopiable pages: Template for a finger puppet (CD-ROM only), Template for a glove puppet (CD-ROM only)

During these tasks the teacher demonstrates, teaches and shows the children specific skills in both designing and making a puppet. The children will learn how to manipulate, cut, join and finish a range of materials and will apply this knowledge to their ideas for making a puppet.

Although much of the communication of design ideas will be through talking with the children, some drawing, sketching or modelling skills should be taught so that they can clarify their ideas on paper, through the use of paper patterns or through modelling with materials. It is important that these skills are developed progressively through their design and technology experiences. For this project the use of ICT graphics packages are a good way to enable children to model their ideas for their puppet.

The template sheets on the CD-ROM only are to encourage quick mark-making activities that will help children to develop their design and communication skills and to record their 3D modelling activities. These activities are linked to art and design and will support work in that area of the curriculum. Work on observational drawing in art and design can also support elements of design and communication.

Discussion
▶ Show the children the templates of the puppets from the CD-ROM. Ask the children what they think the templates are for. Discuss how many pieces would be needed to create the basic puppet. Ask what features would be needed for a range of characters, for example, a person, a rabbit or a giraffe.
▶ Explain to the children that the template is just a rough outline and that they can change the shape of the puppet as long as they do so outside the template lines.

Activities
▶ Create a template using a graphics package, so that the children can use ICT to create their designs. Many packages allow you to create a template and keep the basic outline. Depending on the software, this is can be done when you save your file. You are asked for a filename and at this point you can define the type of file in the 'Save as' box. Scroll down the list and click on template. This will save the file as a template. When the children use it, they can save it under another file name to their own folder.
▶ Use the template sheets from the CD-ROM for the children to modify and create a paper character. Ask them to create a front and back view. They should cut these out and join front and back pieces together around the outer edges – not the bottom edge. Ask whether they can fit their hand/finger into the paper puppet. Ask questions to see if they understand why they can or cannot get the puppet to fit. For example, you could ask why one child's hand is able to fit inside a certain puppet, but another child's cannot.

MAKING PAPER PATTERNS
It is important to give the children the skills needed to be able to successfully make a puppet that they can use in performance. It is crucial that the children make templates/patterns in order to succeed in creating a puppet that fits. Creating a template/pattern for their own puppet is a skill that will be built upon later in their design and make experience.

Discussion
▶ Ask the children how else they could make a pattern for their design, other than using the

template they used last time. Explain that if they really want to make sure that their puppet will fit their hand, they could use their own hand to create a pattern. Ask for ideas on how they might do this.

Activity

▶ Give all the children a piece of squared paper. Ask them to draw around their own hand. They will need to separate their thumb and little finger from the middle three fingers, as in the illustration below. If this is difficult they can work in pairs and draw around each other's hands. Ask the children to draw another line around the outline of their hand about two finger widths further out. Explain that this is to give enough material to go around the width of their hand and to create a seam.

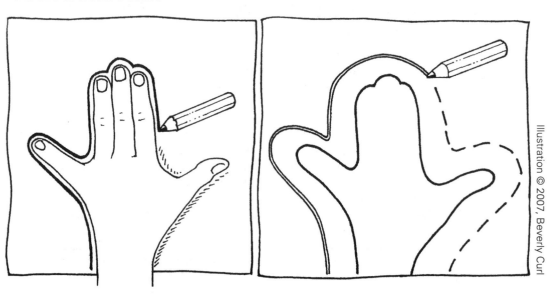

Illustration © 2007, Beverly Curl

CREATING THE CRITERIA

Photographs: Finger puppets, Glove puppet — old man, Glove puppets — crocodile and zebra, Glove puppets — girl and wizard, Indonesian puppet, Pop-up puppets, Sock puppet, Stick puppet, String puppet

Photocopiable page: Planning my design   PAGE 29

This activity is to help the children understand the importance of deciding on what design criteria are needed in their ideas and the product they are going to make. This will be a crucial part of the design and make activity that they go on to complete.

Discussing the photographs

▶ Show the children a variety of puppet photographs from the gallery. Ask them why each puppet is made the way it is. Ask why they think that a particular puppet has big eyes or a big nose, or why they think a particular puppet is small. Discuss the fact that these features were identified by the maker of the puppet as being important to represent the character and tell the story; these features are the *criteria* the designer identified before making the puppet.

Activity

▶ In groups, ask the children to decide which nursery rhyme or story they are going to perform. Ask them to decide which characters they will need to make in to puppets. As a group, they should then decide which child will make which character. Ask individuals to decide what features their character will need in order to make it easy for the audience to know who they are (perhaps a hat, big ears, and so on). Encourage the children to record their ideas on the 'Planning my design' photocopiable on page 29.

SIMPLE SEWING

Video: Running stitch

Photocopiable page: Recording sheet for stitching PAGE 30

This activity gives children the opportunity to learn how to sew two pieces of fabric together, and to experiment with different types of stitching.

Discussion
▶ Ask the children how they think they can connect their two pieces of fabric. When sewing is mentioned, ask how many types of stitch they know. Concentrate on the most useful of these (running stitch, backstitch, oversew stitch) and discuss what each is used for.
▶ Watch the video 'Running stitch' to ensure the children know how to sew fabric together using running stitch.

Activity
▶ Give the children two small fabric squares each and show them how to hold the fabric together using bulldog clips. Make sure that they understand that they need right sides together for running stitch and backstitch, and wrong sides together for oversew stitch. Encourage the children to practise the stitch they wish to use and attached samples of work to the 'Recording sheet for stitching' photocopiable on page 30. They could add this sheet of stitching samples to their process diaries.

DESIGN AND MAKE ACTIVITY

DESIGN AND MAKE A PUPPET

Photocopiable pages: Planning my design, Planning, How I will make my puppet PAGES 29, 31, 32

Explain to the children that they are going to use all the knowledge and understanding from the previous activities to design and make a puppet that is to be used in a performance to help tell a story. They will probably be working in groups to produce puppets for all the main characters in a particular story. They will need to focus on the user and the need for an appropriately sized puppet to suit the type of performance intended (purpose).

The preceding focused practical tasks (FPTs) and investigating and evaluating activities (IEAs) will have taken the children through activities that support elements of the designing and making process. These activities will now be used in the design and make activity to generate ideas and apply knowledge and the practical skills learned to make their final design. These activities are crucial for a successful outcome for the children.

Discussion
▶ A visit to a museum where there is a range of puppets, or a puppeteer visiting the school are good ways to begin this activity or, indeed, the chapter. Make sure that you discuss with the children the purpose of the visit beforehand, so that they know what to look out for when they get there. They could look out for particular types of puppets and jot down ideas for their own creations.
▶ Discuss with the children the requirements for their performance. They need to design and make puppets to enact their story or nursery rhyme. By identifying this need the children can then consider the venue and the type of performance when planning the different types of puppets they could make. Emphasise the need for puppets to be fit for purpose (as discovered throughout the investigating and evaluating activities). The children will need to come up with their own ways to achieve this.
▶ Ask the children which they think is the most appropriate type of puppet needed for the performance. Remind them of what they found out, for example, do they think the audience would be able to see finger puppets from the back of the hall?
▶ Explain to the children that they are going to perform their puppet show to an audience (this could be another class, different groups in the class or school assembly). Explain that

they will need to use what they have learned to design and make a puppet that will be appropriate for their audience. Explain that although they will be working in small groups some of the time, they will all design and make a puppet.

Activities

▶ In groups, the children need to decide which story or play they are going to perform, and which character they will each be making. Discuss what features the puppet might need depending on the character. Ask the children to think about what they found out in the investigating and evaluating activities and focused practical tasks, to help them decide what their puppet will need to look like, where it will be used, the type of puppet to be made and what fabric they want to use. The children could record some of these design decisions on the 'Planning my design' photocopiable on page 29.

▶ Ask the children to look back at what they identified in the 'Creating the criteria' focused practical task. Ask them to draw or make a mock up of a puppet that includes everything they have decided their puppet will need. Ask them to draw their final design for their puppet on a piece of paper and add this work to their process diaries.

▶ Explain to the children that they now need to plan the making of their puppet. They need to identify the fabric and components they want to use and the main stages of making. They can use the 'Planning' photocopiable on page 31 to list the equipment and stages needed in the making and the 'How will I make the puppet' photocopiable page on page 32 to add in their pattern and samples of the fabric. This activity should take place after the children have gone through all the investigating and evaluating and focused practical tasks. This part of the activity links well with writing instructions.

EVALUATION

Photocopiable page: Evaluating   PAGE 33

It is important to allow time for the children to evaluate their own puppet and those made by their peers. This activity supports children in assessing their own learning and progress.

Discussion

▶ Display all the finished puppets that the children have made. Do the children feel that the puppets fulfil the brief? *Are they all suitable for the audience they were created for?* Discuss with the children the importance of using their criteria to evaluate the puppets.

▶ Ask the children to look at the 'Evaluating' photocopiable on page 33, which is based on a rating of happy (smiley face), okay, or not happy (sad face). The evaluation is based on the criteria the children had planned for their puppet to include. It is important that the children are allowed to express their feelings about their finished product but make sure that they understand that the criteria for making are crucial in design and technology evaluations.

Activities

▶ Ask the children to use page 33 to decide how well their designs meet each of the criteria. Ask them to fill in the smiley face evaluation sheet.

▶ The children can then gain the audience's opinion of their puppet by asking two audience members to complete the evaluation chart.

Photograph © 2007, Early Learning Centre

Investigating puppets

▲ Draw and label one of the puppets you have been shown.

1. Which materials is it made from?

2. How are the materials joined together?

3. Who has this puppet been made for?

4. What are the main features of this puppet?

5. Where would you use this puppet?

PUPPETS

Evaluating puppets

▲ Which puppets could you use in each place? Circle one face.

Puppet	Reading area	Role-play area	Hall	Other
	😊 🙂 🙁 ☹	😊 🙂 🙁 ☹	😊 🙂 🙁 ☹	😊 🙂 🙁 ☹
	😊 🙂 🙁 ☹	😊 🙂 🙁 ☹	😊 🙂 🙁 ☹	😊 🙂 🙁 ☹
	😊 🙂 🙁 ☹	😊 🙂 🙁 ☹	😊 🙂 🙁 ☹	😊 🙂 🙁 ☹

Illustration © Beverly Curl

28

READY RESOURCES ▶▶ DESIGN AND TECHNOLOGY

SCHOLASTIC
PHOTOCOPIABLE

Planning my design

▲ I am going to design and make a puppet for _____

(for example for a show for the Reception class / to illustrate a nursery rhyme)

▲ My puppet is going to be _____ (character)

from _____ (nursery rhyme or story)

▲ I want my puppet to have _____

▲ A good puppet should:

1. _____

2. _____

3. _____

4. _____

Recording sheet for stitching

Type of stitch	Sample
Running stitch 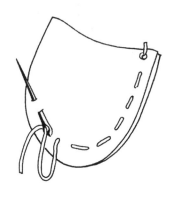	
Backstitch 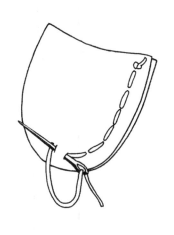	
Oversew stitch 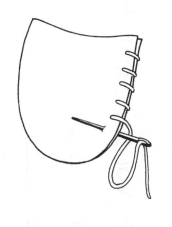	

Illustration © Beverly Curl

📖 SCHOLASTIC
PHOTOCOPIABLE

Planning

▶ What will you need to make your puppet?

▶ List the items here:

1. _____

_____

2. _____

_____

3. _____

_____

4. _____

_____

5. _____

_____

6. _____

_____

▶ How will you make your puppet?

▶ List the main instructions here:

1. _____

_____

2. _____

_____

3. _____

_____

4. _____

_____

5. _____

_____

6. _____

_____

sequins
needle
plastic tubing
hole punch
dowel rod
felt-tipped pens
glue
pegs
card
stapler
sock
yogurt pot
paper plate
cardboard box
sticky tape
fabric
beads
thread
cotton reels
scissors

How I will make my puppet

▲ What materials will you use? (List or stick samples here):

▲ If you make a paper pattern stick it here:

Evaluating

You said you wanted your design to do these things (copy your design criteria here):	How well does your puppet do each of these things?	Audience member 1	Audience member 2
1. _____	:) :) :) :) / :| :| :| :| / :| :| :| :| / :(:(:(:(	:) :) :) :) / :| :| :| :| / :| :| :| :| / :(:(:(:(	:) :) :) :) / :| :| :| :| / :| :| :| :| / :(:(:(:(
2. _____			
3. _____			
4. _____			

| What do you or the audience member think about your design overall? | :) | :| | :| | :(| :) | :| | :| | :(| :) | :| | :| | :(|

▲ What new skills have you learned?

▲ How well did you organise your work?

MOVING PICTURES

Content and skills

The chapter links to Unit 1A 'Moving Pictures' of the QCA Scheme of Work for design and technology at Key Stage 1. It focuses on mechanisms made with paper and card to make an illustration more interactive and interesting for a specific purpose and user.

The chapter encourages the children to look at a range of books, greeting cards and information boards that have moving parts, in order to understand how they work and why using movement enhances these products. The children will be encouraged to discuss how each mechanism works and is constructed.

The children will be developing their understanding of how to make pictures move using levers and sliders. This work is the basis for developing an understanding of mechanical control.

The children will have opportunities to learn that simple levers and sliding mechanisms can be used to create movement and that this movement needs to be controlled. They will explore and evaluate the use of levers in everyday products around them, for example, scissors and will learn and use new vocabulary associated with mechanisms, such as, *pivot*, *levers*, *sliders*, *directions*. They will also explore construction kits to develop their understanding of mechanisms. For the main activity, they will design and make a product using simple sliding and lever mechanisms. Throughout they will be using tools safely and effectively, for example, a hole-punch and a paper drill.

The chapter is structured as follows:
▶ Investigating and evaluating: existing products with mechanisms.
▶ Making illustrations move.
▶ Making sliders.
▶ Making simple levers.
▶ Design and communication.
▶ Design and make activity.
▶ Evaluating their moving pictures.

Outcome

The main outcome for this chapter will be for the children to design and make an illustration that has a moving element, to make a product such as a class or group book, a greeting card, an information board or a display more interactive. In doing this, the children will be expected to:
▶ investigate and evaluate a range of illustrations and objects with moving parts
▶ use tools safely to make a moving picture that incorporates a simple lever or slider
▶ use one of the taught techniques to practise their making skills and as a starting point for developing their own ideas
▶ talk about the reason there are moving illustrations in books, greetings cards and other paper/card products
▶ discuss who they are going to design their moving picture for and identify what it needs to do
▶ be able to talk about how simple moving products work.

Health and safety

In this chapter the children will be learning skills in cutting and they will be using scissors frequently. Ensure that children carry scissors closed with blades in their palms. Refer to your school and local authority health and safety policies and guidelines on the use of sharp equipment.

Links to other subjects

English: Skills such as questioning, describing, speaking and listening are needed when carrying out the activities. The children will have opportunities to read words related to work on mechanisms, tools and equipment and should be encouraged to use the correct terminology at all times. There are opportunities for writing their own captions to go with their moving picture or to improvise or role play the intended movement of their design. The children could read one another's stories or follow instructions to make a product.

Organising the unit

All elements of the unit should be covered but the order in which they are covered can be of your own choosing. For example, starting points could be:

▶ a focused practical task where the children are shown how to make a slider, and then the investigation and evaluation activities can be used to help the children see where slider mechanisms are used in other products

▶ reading the same story from two different books – one with moving illustrations and one without and then discussing with the children which book they liked the best and why

▶ investigating the class collection of products with moving parts.

The children can work in small groups to create one book, with each child producing a moving illustration. Alternatively, they can work individually to create a greeting card or an information board.

Resources on the CD-ROM

Videos on the CD-ROM demonstrate the different products that use mechanisms to create movement, for example, a see-saw and a lever door handle. The products are shown working, so the children can see and understand the type of movement that is created. Encourage the children to note whether is it forwards, backwards, up, down, and so on.

Photocopiable pages

The photocopiable sheets in the book and on the CD-ROM include:

▶ a worksheet showing everyday objects that have a lever mechanism for the children to discuss and annotate

▶ design and planning sheets for the children to use to build up a process diary for the chapter

▶ examples of moving pictures that use levers or sliders to create a pop-up movement (these can be used in conjunction with the examples collected by the class).

Photocopiable resources on the CD-ROM only include support sheets for teaching practical skills and advice on safe use of tools. Key vocabulary word cards are also provided.

INVESTIGATING AND EVALUATING IDEAS

EXISTING PRODUCTS WITH MECHANISMS

Videos: Lever door handle, See-saw

Photocopiable pages: Objects with moving parts, Moving pictures, Names of tools (CD-ROM only), Word cards: moving pictures (CD-ROM only)

PAGES 41–42

Make sure that you give the children the opportunity to explore and evaluate existing products that demonstrate different types of movement. The children need to understand that it is mechanisms that create different types of movement.

Ask the children to consider the users and purposes of each product. They should be encouraged to identify the type of movement in each example and to explain how they think it works. Then, give them the opportunity to look around the classroom and school to see if they can identify objects that use mechanisms to create movement.

Discussing the videos

▶ Use the videos to show the mechanisms in the see-saw and lever door handle. Ask the children if they can tell which mechanism has been used and what movement it creates.

▶ Use the video clips and the 'Objects with moving parts' photocopiable on page 41 to identify different types of movement. Ask questions about which part is moving, how it works, and what makes it move in that particular way. Do the children think it is effective?

▶ Talk about the fact that mechanisms make things move forwards, backwards, up, down, left and right. Encourage the children to identify what needs to happen for the mechanism to work – for example, pull the slider (input) for the linear motion to happen (output), push a lever down (input) for the see-saw mechanism to go up in an arc or oscillating movement (output). See the 'Moving pictures' photocopiable page 42 for examples of different pop-up movements.

Activities

▶ Ask the children questions about some hands-on products in the classroom. Examples of levers in everyday use might include scissors, a door handle, a stapler. Sliders in everyday use could include a draw, a box pencil case that slides to open, a hatch in the dinner hall or the office. In each case, ask what the moving part does, how it works, what effect it has and whether it works well. Can they see how the parts are joined together? How could they use this to help with their own design ideas?

▶ Discuss the tools that the children will need, using the 'Names of tools' sheet from the CD-ROM.

▶ Use the 'Words cards: moving pictures' sheet from CD-ROM to familiarise the children with the key vocabulary.

▶ Use the collection of examples found in the classroom or those the children have brought from home and investigate how they are made. Ask questions about what materials have been used to make each product and how the parts are joined together.

Type of motion	Description of motion	
Linear motion	Linear motion is motion in a straight line.	
Reciprocating motion	Reciprocating motion is linear motion going backwards and forwards	
Rotary motion	Rotary motion is motion that is circular	
Oscillating motion	Oscillating motion is forward and backward motion in a circular arc	

MAKING ILLUSTRATIONS MOVE

Illustrations: Hey Diddle Diddle, Hansel and Gretel, Little Red Riding Hood, Car, Train, Beach, Crab

The illustrations on the CD-ROM include well-known characters from nursery rhymes, traditional tales and pictures that would link to other topics, for example, the seaside and vehicles. The children should consider how to make the illustrations more engaging by making them move, but they should be encouraged to consider carefully which is the most appropriate part to move: for example, making the jaws of the wolf move would emphasise how fierce the wolf is, while making the basket swing would not support the ideas or characters of the story.

Discussing the photographs

▶ Discuss with the children why a moving picture is used in a product. What do they think the purpose is – to make the book interactive and interesting for the reader, to help children to predict what comes next, and so on. What do they think the moving part brings to the illustration? Why do they think moving parts are used in books and greetings cards?

▶ Show 'Hey Diddle Diddle' and discuss how this illustration could be made more interesting by adding moving parts. There is only one real option here, which is to use a lever to make the cow jump over the moon.

▶ Show 'Hansel and Gretel' and 'Little Red Riding Hood' and discuss how there are different options for making these pictures move. Hansel and Gretel could move up the path or the cat could move along the side of the house; the wolf's jaws could open and close or Red Riding Hood's arm could move. Discuss various ideas and decide which are best. Encourage the children to think about what the most important part of the picture is, and what would move in reality (it would be more appropriate to move the cat than the chimney pot, for example).

You may want to repeat the discussion for 'Car', 'Train', 'Beach' and 'Crab', particularly if these fit in to topics the class is currently studying.

Activities

▶ Give the children a product and ask them to draw it, showing how it moves. Show them how to label the parts on their design.

▶ Share a few examples of good drawings with the class. Ask them if the design clearly shows how the mechanism works. How could the design be improved? How could they use this to help with their own design ideas?

FOCUSED PRACTICAL TASKS

MAKING SLIDERS

Photocopiable pages: Moving pictures, My design ideas PAGES 42–43

During this section the children will learn how to make their own sliders using card and construction kits.

Discussion

▶ Using an existing product, ask the children to predict what will happen if a slider is pulled.

For example, ask: *What will happen if I slide this? How can I make the clown's hat lift off?*
▶ Ask the children to look at the diagrams of sliders at the top of the 'Moving pictures' photocopiable on page 42. Discuss and then demonstrate how to make sliding mechanisms using the hole-punch and double-sided sticky pads. They can use the 'My design ideas' photocopiable page 43 to record their ideas.

Activities
▶ Use a range of kits and other construction materials to allow the children to model their ideas. The children could print a picture using clip art and stick it onto the moving part.
▶ Allow the children opportunities to design and make their own sliders and levers using card. Make sure that sticky tape, masking tape, sticky pads, scissors and so on are available to the children so they can make their own choices.
▶ Have some card strips readily available for the children to use.
▶ Tell the children that they can print images off the computer or draw their own to use on their models.
▶ Allow the children plenty of time to practise using the hole-punch or a paper drill over a piece of wood (to make a hole in a larger piece of card.) Ensure that the children have plenty of practice at punching holes accurately.
▶ Ask the children to make a slider that goes up and down (for example, a hat on a clown) and one that moves along (for example, a car on a road). Ask them to evaluate how well the sliders worked. Can the children suggest any improvements?
▶ Teach the children how to restrict the amount of movement made by sliders, using strips of card.

MAKING SIMPLE LEVERS

Photocopiable pages: Moving pictures, My design ideas PAGES 42–43

Discussion
▶ Ask children to look at the bottom of the sheet 'Moving pictures' on page 42. Discuss how they might go about making a simple lever and what they would need to use. They can use the 'My design ideas' photocopiable on page 43 to record their ideas
▶ Discuss and then demonstrate how to make levers and explain what happens if the paper fastener is too tight. Remind the children how to use the hole-punch safely.

Activities
▶ The children use paper fasteners to make a lever. Ask the children what happens if the fasteners are too tight or too loose? Do they think the fasteners worked effectively? Why? How do they think it could be improved?
▶ Ask the children to share their work with the class. Talk about how they made their levers and any problems they had to overcome. Evaluate as a class.

DESIGN AND COMMUNICATION

Photocopiable pages: Make the aeroplane move,
Moving pictures, Developing my design PAGES 42, 44, 45

Although much of the communication of design ideas will be through talking with the children, some drawing, sketching or modelling skills should be taught. The children could be given opportunity to communicate and clarify their ideas on paper, through the use of construction kits or through modelling with materials. It is important that these skills are developed progressively through their design and technology experiences.

Discussion
▶ Show the children the 'Make the aeroplane move' on page 44. Talk about the type of motion that will be created. Point out the direction arrow. (This reinforces the Investigation and evaluation activity). Explain that this is a good way to indicate what movement they want on a drawing.

Activities

▶ Ask the children to think of all the possible ways they could make the aeroplane picture move. They could respond by drawing onto the sheet or by cutting out and sticking the aeroplane (photocopied on card) onto recycled packaging to make mock-ups showing how the plane would move. Ask the children to show you how their aeroplane will move, and look at the 'Moving pictures' photocopiable page 42 for ideas.

▶ Ask the children to choose another image – a character from a story or a nursery rhyme. They can draw the character using the 'Developing my design' photocopiable on page 45 (less confident learners could use a ready-made image for this activity). Ask them to show what part of the illustration they want to make move and how they think they could achieve this. Again, making mock-ups is a good way to allow children to practise making mechanisms.

DESIGN AND MAKE ACTIVITY

DESIGN AND MAKE A MOVING PICTURE

Photocopiable pages: My design ideas, Developing my design, Word cards: moving pictures (CD-ROM only), My Plan **PAGES 43, 45, 46**

Explain to the children that they are now going to use the knowledge and skills learned in the previous activities to design and make a class book, book page, greeting card or information board that has a moving part, in order to make it more interesting and interactive. The product will be targeted at a specific user, such as visitors to the class for the information board, or perhaps another class for the storybook, or the whole school for an interactive display.

The following are some of the contexts and outcomes that could be used as the design and make activity:

▶ Design and make a moving picture with a particular purpose and user in mind, for example, a picture of a character from a class Big Book to be used by Year 1 pupils.

▶ Design and make a moving picture based on characters or scenes from a Big Book that can be used to liven up the story for the listener. The children can chose their own story or the whole class could work on the same story;

▶ Design and make moving pictures that you can use when reading out your favourite poem.

▶ Design and make an information board for hanging on the classroom door to inform visitors where the class is, and what they are doing.

▶ Design and make an interactive display for the hall to tell all the other classes about a particular subject.

▶ Design and make an information board about a special message, for example recycling of paper, animal welfare, keeping safe, and so on.

Discussion

▶ Explain the design brief to the children. Decide whether the class will be designing and making moving pictures as a whole class on a chosen theme, a Big Book, information board or creating their own special messages. Remind the children that they need to have a clear purpose and a clear user in mind when designing and making their products. Remind the children how to label their designs clearly.

▶ Look at and discuss existing products with moving parts (moving greeting cards, pop-up books, simple levers and sliding mechanisms.) Focus on the purpose and user of each product displayed.

▶ Discuss what their moving picture is for and what it has to do – make a story more interesting, liven up an information board, make a greeting card for a special occasion even more special.

▶ Discuss who will be reading the book or using the board so they can design with the user in mind.

Activities

▶ Use 'My design ideas' photocopiable on page 43 to allow children to think about possible designs and to annotate these clearly to show their intentions. Encourage the children to

evaluate throughout the whole design process. The children then use 'Developing my design' photocopiable on page 45 to describe the final design. They should decide how the illustration will move, draw this and add this to their process diary.

▶ Ask the children to reread their design brief/design specification that clearly states the purpose and user of their moving picture.

▶ Remind the children of the key vocabulary they have learned and encourage them to use the correct terminology. Display the 'Word cards: moving pictures' sheet from the CD-ROM as a prompt.

▶ Ask the children to produce a plan of action, using words and/or pictures to show the order in which they will make their moving picture. They can use the 'My plan' photocopiable on page 46 for this. Allow the children to make paper mock ups if they wish.

▶ Remind the children of the tools, equipment, materials and any constraints. It is advisable to store resources centrally and ensure that they are well labelled. This will encourage independent learning. The children will need to plan the order in which they go about their work before they start making. This will encourage them to think about the tools and equipment they need and the order in which they will make their moving picture. They can use words or pictures to plan their work.

▶ Allow time for the children to complete their pictures. Remind them to work cooperatively. They should be evaluating throughout the whole design process, and referring to their final design and planning sheet. Their final product should look like their design. Any changes or modifications should be noted. Ensure, however, that children realise that they can change their design as they develop their ideas.

▶ When the children have finished, they should draw the final product and record how it moves and add this to their process diaries.

▶ Ask the children to think about finishing techniques, such as collage, paint, felts, and so on.

▶ Take photographs of the pictures in progress as this can support the children in their evaluations and be used for display or evidence.

EVALUATION

Photocopiable page: My Evaluation   PAGE 47

The evaluation activity is an opportunity for the children to present their moving pictures to the rest of the class and to evaluate their own and others' work.

Discussion
▶ Display all the moving pictures that the class has made.
▶ Ask children to share their work with the class, talking about who the product was made for and how it works. Evaluate these as a class. Does the product fulfil the design criteria?

Activities
▶ Encourage the children to evaluate their work and that of others using the 'Evaluation' photocopiable on page 47. Ask them to think about how the product works and whether it is effective? Did their illustration move in the right direction? Did it work the way they thought it would? Do they think it meets the design brief? Do they think it linked in well with the story? Is their finishing technique effective? What would they change to improve it? Do they think there is anything that could be added to make it better? How did they overcome difficulties or problems?

▶ If their products were made for a class big book, read the book and allow the children to test out the product as a whole. *Do the moving pictures make the story more interesting? Which products work well? How do they move? Who used levers? Who used sliders? Did we design and make a product for a particular purpose? What? Did we design and make a product for a particular user? Who?*

Objects with moving parts

▶ How do these objects move? (Add labels.)

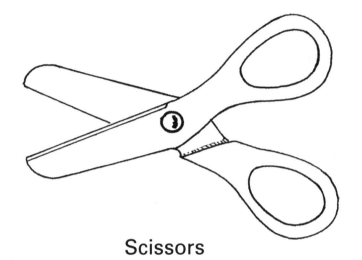

Scissors

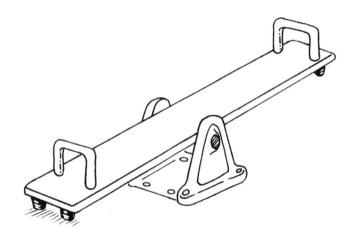

See-saw

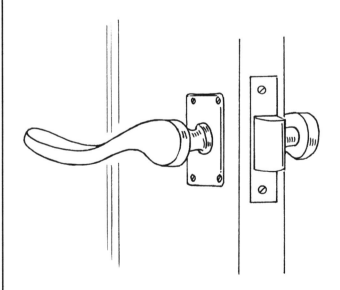

Lever door handle

◖SCHOLASTIC
PHOTOCOPIABLE

Moving pictures

▶ Draw arrows to show how these pictures move.
▶ One has been done for you.

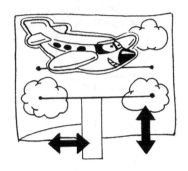

1.

2.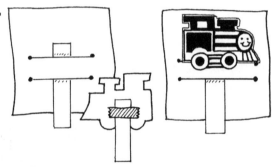

3.

4.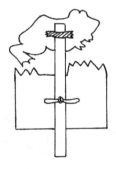

◣ SCHOLASTIC
PHOTOCOPIABLE

My design ideas

▶ Draw your ideas here and label them carefully.

Make the aeroplane move

► Here is one idea for making an aeroplane move:

► Can you think of two other ideas?
► Add your ideas to the pictures below.

■ SCHOLASTIC
PHOTOCOPIABLE

Illustration © Beverly Curl

Developing my design

▶ Sketch or stick the picture you want to use for your illustration below.

▶ Show what type of mechanism you want to use.

▶ Show how it will move.

My plan

▶ Use words and pictures to show how you will make your product.

My evaluation

My plan was to: _____

_____

_____

_____

_____

I am happy with: _____

_____

_____

_____

_____

The problems I solved were: _____

_____

_____

_____

_____

Next time I would: _____

_____

_____

_____

_____

PLAYGROUNDS

Content and skills

This chapter links to Unit 1B 'Playgrounds' of the QCA Scheme of Work for design and technology at Key Stage 1. The chapter focuses on framework structures used in play equipment and their users.

Photograph © eb33 / iStockphoto.com

In this chapter the children will be challenged to design and make a model of a piece of playground equipment which will be useable by children with a specific disability.

This will encourage children to look at a range of full-sized play equipment, talk about who would use the equipment, who might not be able to use the equipment and to make suggestions as to modifications for those not able to use the equipment. They are encouraged to think about the wide range of users of the playground; that all children play and that play equipment can be designed for many needs. (These include children who may be blind or partially sighted, deaf or hard of hearing.) The key message that this chapter develops is that design should include everyone. People may have different abilities but many of their needs are the same.

The children will have opportunities to learn about framework structures, shell structures, how to make frameworks stable and able to support loads. They will investigate materials used for the play equipment and how the play equipment is assembled.

Through a range of focused tasks they will develop skills in designing in 3D using construction kits and construction materials (mock-ups). They will use construction kits to model their initial ideas, combining kits with reclaimed materials to develop their ideas, creative design skills, evaluation skills and practical making skills.

The chapter is structured as follows:
▶ Investigating and evaluating: playground equipment.
▶ Design and communication.
▶ Generating ideas.
▶ Developing ideas.
▶ Practical skills.
▶ How to make things stand up and be stable.
▶ Design and make activity.
▶ Evaluating their model playground equipment.

Outcome

The main outcome of this chapter will be for children to design and make a model of an item of playground equipment, for example, a swing, roundabout, climbing frame or adventure playground equipment.

In doing this, the children will be expected to:
▶ investigate a range of actual items of playground equipment and consider how they are suitable for all users
▶ join construction kit components together and combine them with other materials, for example, card, reclaimed materials, dowelling and string
▶ successfully construct a realistic model of an item of playground equipment
▶ assemble their model with accuracy and be able to talk about how it is appropriate for the intended user.

Health and safety

During this chapter the children will be using tools such as a junior hacksaw, paper drill and scissors. Make sure that you refer to your school and local authority health and safety policies and guidelines, for the safe use of sharp tools and any other equipment.

Links to other subjects

English: The activities provide opportunities for the children to use skills such as questioning, describing, speaking and listening. For example, children comparing two items of play equipment will need to be able to observe and identify similarities and differences in the characteristics of the equipment through talk. When investigating and evaluating play equipment, they will be posing questions to evaluate the play equipment.

Organising the unit

All three types of activity should be covered but the order in which they are covered can be of your own choosing. For example, starting points could be:
▶ a visit to the local play area, taking photographs to use later
▶ the focused practical tasks which covers making things stand up and the structure being stable
▶ discussing the video clip of a group of children in a playground, using the equipment.

Resources on the CD-ROM

The CD-ROM contains images of play equipment in playgrounds from public spaces and schools, including equipment for children with disabilities. These images are intended to supplement photographs taken on a class visit to the local play space where the children explore the equipment first hand. These photographs can then be looked at, discussed and evaluated with different users in mind.

There is also a video clip of a group of children using a playground, with some of the children not being able to use the rides. This can stimulate a discussion about what makes the playground accessible to children and the reasons why some children may not be able to take part.

Photocopiable pages

The photocopiable sheets in the book and on the CD-ROM include:
▶ several sheets for teachers to make interactive displays to use in classroom to support the discussions about users
▶ a series of worksheets for children to record their design ideas which can be adapted for different contexts and put together to form a process diary
▶ support sheets for teaching practical skills for mark making.

There are also photocopiables on the CD-ROM only which include word lists to aid vocabulary development and general sheets of advice on the safe use of tools.

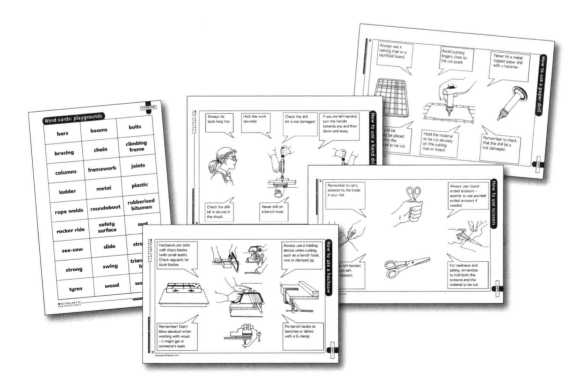

INVESTIGATING AND EVALUATING IDEAS

PLAYGROUND EQUIPMENT

Photographs: Spring ride, Spring ride – see-saw, Swings, Swing seat, Climbing equipment 1, Climbing equipment 2, Roundabout, Grass protection mats, Loose fill surfacing, Wet fill surfacing, Wheelchair roundabout, Infant car seat, Wheelchair ramp
Video: Children's playground

Photocopiable pages: Word cards: playgrounds (CD-ROM only), Investigating play equipment, Evaluating play equipment, Comparing two swings   **PAGES 55-57**

Make sure that the children are able to explore and evaluate large play equipment through a visit to a local play area. Follow this up using photographs taken during the visit and the photographs from the CD-ROM to stimulate discussion. During these activities the need for changes to the equipment, so that all children can play, will become apparent. Looking at the materials used and how the equipment has been constructed will help to develop the children's understanding of how the structures are able to stand upright and be strong enough to climb on. It is through these activities that the children will be able to identify the criteria needed for their ideas, when designing for everyone. They will use these criteria to generate and develop their ideas.

Discussing the photographs
▶ Show the photographs 'Spring ride', 'Spring ride– see-saw' 'Swings' and 'Swing seat' and discuss which are for toddlers and which are for older children: how do they know? (The spring ride and swing seat have bars and/or high sides to stop toddlers falling off.) Show the photographs of the two climbing frames and discuss the different users, as above. (One is for older children, and requires balancing skills, while the other is for younger children as it has higher sides.)
▶ Look again at the photographs above, and the 'Roundabout'. Discuss the materials the equipment is made from and how the different rides move. Encourage the children to consider how movement is influenced by the intended user (something that spins very fast would be for an older child, compared with the spring ride, which moves very gently).
▶ Use the photographs to discuss the structure of the equipment and how it is made stable and stronger. Point out the features of the swings – the framework is an A-frame and the A-frame base is buried in the ground to secure it so that it will not move when children use the swings. (This will be the same for many of the pieces of playground equipment.)
▶ Discuss safety features on the ground, using the photographs of different surfacing, 'Grass protection mats', 'Loose fill surfacing' and 'Wet fill surfacing'. Explore why these surfaces are there in place and how they would feel.
▶ Show the wheelchair roundabout and discuss how this is different to the other roundabout (there is a large area in the centre of the roundabout for a wheelchair; there is not much space in the centre of the roundabout in the other photograph as metal bars are in the way).
▶ Use the photographs 'Infant car seat' and 'Wheelchair ramp' to discuss their purpose and whether they could be used to adapt different types of play equipment to allow all children to use it.
▶ Look again at the swings and spring ride photographs: can the children think of any ways to adapt these for wheelchair users?

Discussing the video
▶ Show the video 'Children's playground' and discuss why the children are able to use some but not all of the equipment (sometimes the children are too big or too small).
▶ Ask the children whether a wheelchair user would be able to use any of this equipment: do they think this fair?

Activities

▶ Use the 'Word cards: playgrounds' sheet from the CD-ROM to familiarise the children with the main words associated with structures, and play equipment.

▶ Ask the children to record their evaluations of the equipment in the photographs on the 'Investigating play equipment', 'Evaluating play equipment' and 'Comparing two swings' photocopiable pages on pages 55–57.

FOCUSED PRACTICAL TASKS

DESIGN AND COMMUNICATION

Photocopiable page: Making marks   PAGE 58

This focused practical task teaches some drawing and modelling skills. Explain to the children that they will be communicating and clarifying their ideas on paper using drawing, through the use of construction kits, or through modelling with materials. These skills will be developed progressively through their design and technology experiences. For this project, the use of appropriate construction kits (with other construction materials) and digital cameras are a good way of quickly modelling and recording ideas.

Discussion

▶ Show the children the range of construction kits available. Discuss with them what they are designed to do. Which kit would they use to make a climbing frame? Why? Which kit is best to make a roundabout? Why? How do they think they could connect the pieces?

▶ Discuss what might be missing from their models if they just used a construction kit. Ask the children what other materials could be used with the kit – for example, string, small boxes, cardboard, Plasticine®.

Activities

▶ Use the 'Making marks' photocopiable on page 58 to encourage quick mark-making activities that will help the children to develop their design and communication skills and to record their 3D modelling activities. These activities are linked to art and design and will support work in that area of the curriculum. Work on observational drawing in art and design will also support elements of design and communication.

▶ Use construction kits that support learning about framework structures to demonstrate how to make models of existing play equipment.

▶ Ask the children to communicate their ideas on paper by drawing their construction kit model.

▶ Using a range of kits and other construction materials, encourage the children to model play equipment.

GENERATING IDEAS

Photographs: Infant car seat, Roundabout, Swings

Photocopiable page: My design ideas   PAGE 59

The 'My design ideas' photocopiable on page 59 will provide the children with strategies to think of creative solutions and record their ideas for the play equipment. The sheet is just one way of presenting these activities to the children. These activities can be used on the interactive whiteboard with the whole class or copied onto A1 paper for small-group work.

Encourage the children to let their imaginations go for a walk – allow all their ideas to be voiced regardless of whether they will be able to realise them or not. This is an opportunity for the children to be creative and think – without you setting any constraints. In the third focused practical task, 'Developing ideas', the constraints for making will be applied and some ideas will then be eliminated. For some children, thinking creatively comes naturally, for others you will need to provide strategies for developing this type of thinking. These activities need to be taught, just as the practical skills are taught, and then reinforced and consolidated. Once learned, these strategies will become part of the children's design thinking.

For example, 'deconstruct to reconstruct' is a strategy where you look at features of two different products and then take features from both and build them into a new idea to solve problems or fulfil specific needs.

Discussing the photographs

▶ Use the method called 'deconstruct to re-construct'. Look at the photograph of the 'Infant car seat' and identify the features and what they are for. Can the children explain why the seat has straps? Why is it that shape?

▶ Repeat the activity using the picture of the 'Roundabout' or 'Swings' and identify what is missing for users with disabilities.

▶ Use two items (the car seat and either the swing or roundabout) to discuss with the children how features from both could be incorporated into their ideas for a new type of play equipment. Look at the car seat and discuss what is special about the chair, how the baby stays in safely, why there is a lining and why it is this shape. Next, look at the swings or roundabout and discuss what needs to be done to allow all children to play on it. Ask how it could be made safe and how this equipment could be adapted for a wheelchair user.

Activities

▶ Encourage the children to decide who they are going to design a piece of play equipment for – a visually or hearing-impaired person or a wheelchair user, what piece of play equipment they are going to think about and what the play equipment will need to have for their chosen user. Encourage them to record their ideas by modelling with construction kits, simple drawing and sketches or through the use of photographic images and annotation. This relates to the criteria-setting part of the design and make activity.

DEVELOPING IDEAS

Photocopiable sheets: Developing ideas 1, Developing ideas 2

PAGES 60–61

Many children start off with one idea, right at the beginning of the project and stick with it so that this is the solution they produce. This activity helps children to use the criteria they have decided on to evaluate these first ideas. They will then able to choose the best features from each initial idea and combine them to produce the best idea that they can.

Discussion

▶ Discuss the first method of developing ideas, by looking at the criteria decided upon and then evaluating ideas against them, using the 'Developing ideas 1' photocopiable on page 60. Developing one idea is sometimes more manageable for some children than trying to create another idea.

▶ Show the 'Developing ideas 2' photocopiable on page 61. Explain to the children that in this second method, everyone looks at one initial idea to help it grow and move forward (method is based on DeBono's green hat theory). Explain to the children that everyone is going to think positively to look for all the ways to take ideas further, making suggestions for modifications and variations. The children should make a special effort to be creative. Ask the children if they think this is better or worse than the first method.

Activities

▶ The children use the sheet 'Developing ideas 2' to look at someone else's initial ideas and evaluate against the criteria that have been set. They will identify what needs to be changed and what are good elements of the idea. Encourage the children to show their changes on their drawings, or print-outs of digital camera images

▶ Ask the children to look at each other's ideas and complete the sheet. As with the creative design strategy in the focused practical task 'Generating ideas', the children will find this easier the more times they are taken through the process.

PRACTICAL SKILLS

Photocopiable pages: How to use a hacksaw (CD-ROM only), How to use a hand drill (CD-ROM only), How to use a paper drill (CD-ROM only), How to use scissors (CD-ROM only), Joining materials **PAGE 62**

These focused tasks are important in that they allow children to learn about how materials are cut, shaped, joined and finished. The is key to the children being able to successfully realise their design ideas as 3D representations. They should learn about how to use and transport the tools safely and how to minimise risks to themselves and to other children.

Discussion

▶ Discuss which tools the children will need to use to realise their design ideas: a hacksaw, scissors, a hand drill, a paper drill. Ask the children what the dangers of using such equipment might be. What can they do to minimise these dangers? Display the relevant sheets from the CD-ROM and make sure they understand how to use the tools safely.

▶ Review the joining techniques from the 'Joining materials' photocopiable on page 62. Discuss with the children which joining techniques would be suitable for the models they plan to make.

▶ Discuss how they might finish their model, and what techniques they might use. What will they need to complete their product?

Activities

▶ Demonstrate to the children how to cut card and hold scissors so accurate cutting can be carried out.

▶ Demonstrate how to hold and use a hacksaw safely, using a bench hook which is securely clamped to a worktop.

▶ Demonstrate how to use a hand drill, using a wood vice or drilling jig.

▶ Demonstrate some of the joining techniques on page 62.

▶ Demonstrate how to finish a model, for example, painting, cladding with card, finishing card edges with tape.

▶ Under supervision, the children then practise using the equipment to join materials and try out finishing techniques. Circulate and make sure they are doing so safely at all times.

HOW TO MAKE THINGS STAND UP AND BE STABLE?

Photocopiable page: Can Humpty Dumpty stand up? **PAGE 63**

This activity is designed to help children begin to understand that they can make simple structures stand up simply by making their bases wider.

Discussion

▶ Discuss how to make items stand up and be stable. What do they think is required? How might they make an oval shape, like Humpty Dumpty, stand upright?

Activities

▶ This activity can be undertaken by the whole class or in small groups. The children can use 'Can Humpty Dumpty stand up?' photocopiable on page 63 for this. Ask each child to draw and cut out a Humpty Dumpty (egg-shaped). Then challenge them to make Humpty stand up. They are allowed to use card, masking tape and Plasticine®.

▶ Ask the children to share their ideas with the group. You will need to draw out that in successful solutions, the children made the base of the egg-shape wider, in one or more directions.

Illustration © 2007, Beverly Curl

DESIGN AND MAKE ACTIVITY

DESIGN AND MAKE MODEL PLAYGROUND EQUIPMENT

Photocopiable page: My plan   PAGE 64

The children will use all the knowledge from the previous activities to design and create a model piece of playground equipment that will be suitable for children, with and without disabilities, to use.

Set a context for the activity to allow the children to see the purpose for designing and making a model of a piece of playground equipment. There are various ways to do this, for example, tell a story involving a child with a disability; make links with a special school, where there are children with specific needs or visit a local play area and pose some crucial questions: *Could a wheelchair user use the roundabout or swing? How would a visually impaired user know when the roundabout has stopped?*

Discussion

▶ Explain to the children that they are going to choose a child with a disability for whom they will create a new piece of playground equipment. Encourage the children to identify what they want their play equipment to be able to do, what it will be made from and how their chosen user will be able to access the equipment (design criteria).

▶ It is important that the key messages for inclusion in this discussion are highlighted: disability does not equal 'stupidity'; giving people who have restricted abilities the time to do things for themselves, wherever possible, is polite (and is no more than those without disabilities would expect); people with disabilities have feelings and can be hurt and offended by inappropriate behaviour; everyone in life is entitled to an equal opportunity even if it can't always be an 'identical opportunity'.

Activities

▶ Ask the children to plan the making of their playground equipment model. They can use the 'My plan' photocopiable on page 64 to identify the materials they want to use to construct their model and the main stages of making. This should take place after they have gone through the focused practical tasks and investigating and evaluating activities.

▶ Allow the children time to make their model. Remind them of the health and safety issues for using the various equipment. Make sure they consider their plan and user throughout.

▶ When they have finished, ask them to draw their model or take a digital photograph to add to their process diary.

EVALUATION

Photocopiable page: Evaluation   PAGE 65

This activity is to encourage the children to evaluate their finished model and how well it fits with their original criteria for designing and making. It is also an opportunity to reflect on what they have learned and how well they went about their designing and making tasks. This activity supports children to assess their own learning.

Discussion

▶ Display all the finished models and discuss them as a class. Ask individuals to describe their work to the class. How many different techniques have they used?

▶ Discuss with the children the importance of using their original criteria to evaluate their designing and making. Ask them to decide how well their designs meet each of the criteria.

Activity

▶ Ask the children to use the 'Evaluation' photocopiable page 65 to assess their work. This sheet is based on a rating of 'not happy', 'okay' (a choice of two faces) and 'very happy'. It also asks what they like about their model and what they have learned. It is important that the children are allowed to express their feelings about their finished product but the criteria for making are also crucial in design and technology evaluations.

Investigating play equipment

Who would play on this? How do you know?

How old would they be?

What materials could have been used to build this?

Can everyone play on this?

Illustration © Beverly Curl

Evaluating play equipment

Is it fun to play on? How does it work?

How could a child in a wheelchair use a ride like this?

Where do you sit?

Can the user fall off? What can be done to stop the user falling off?

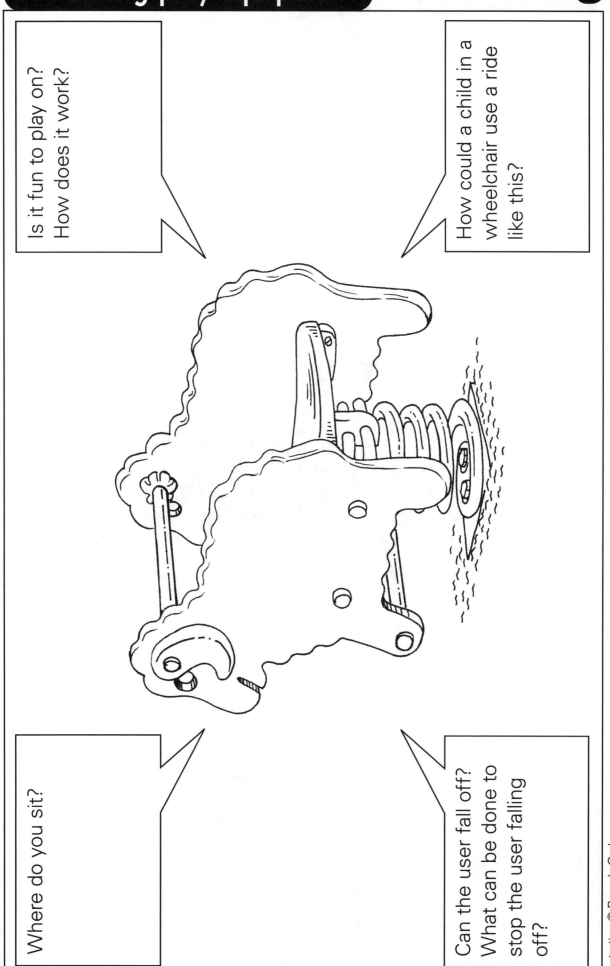

Illustration © Beverly Curl

Comparing two swings

Here are two swings.	What is the same?	What is different?	Why is it different?

Making marks

	Light			Dark
Shading				

Hatching				

Making patterns				

Front view		

Side view		

READY RESOURCES ▶▶ DESIGN AND TECHNOLOGY

My design ideas

My design is for (user) _____

_____

I am going to design and make a model of

_____

_____

I want my play equipment to be (criteria):

1. _____

2. _____

3. _____

My ideas for play equipment look like this:

Developing ideas (1)

My design is for _____ (user)

I am going to design and make a model _____ (product)

How well do your ideas match your criteria?

	Criteria 1 (Write the criteria)	Criteria 2 (Write the criteria)	Criteria 3 (Write the criteria)
Idea 1	:) :) :(:(	:) :) :(:(	:) :) :(:(
Idea 2	:) :) :(:(	:) :) :(:(	:) :) :(:(
Idea 3	:) :) :(:(	:) :) :(:(	:) :) :(:(

Developing ideas (2)

My favourite idea is ⎯⎯⎯⎯⎯⎯⎯⎯⎯⎯⎯

Sketch your best idea here.

Design buddy 1

Make some suggestions to help your friend improve the idea.

Design buddy 2

Make some suggestions to help your friend improve the idea.

Joining materials

▶ You can join straws like this:

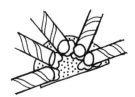
Glue straws to card.

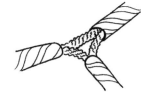
Join with pipe cleaners.

Wrap straws together.

Flatten ends and glue.

▶ You can fix straws like this:

Use sticky tape.

Use Plasticine®.

▶ You can fix seats like this:

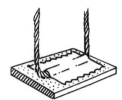
Use tape and cardboard.

Use pipe cleaners.

▶ You can join things with:

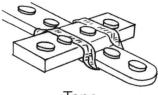
Tape.

Elastic bands.

▶ You can make things more stable like this:

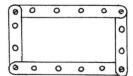
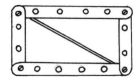
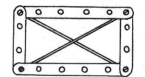

Can Humpty Dumpty stand up?

Draw Humpty Dumpty and cut him out.

You have a piece of card, some strips of card, a small amount of Plasticine®.
Can you make Humpty Dumpty stand up?

My plan

What will you need to make your design?
List the items here. (Use the wordbank to help you.)

▲ ▲

1. _____

2. _____

3. _____

4. _____

5. _____

scissors   wooden wheels   needle   paper drill   pipe cleaners   dowel rod

pegs   stapler   cotton reels   cardboard box   card   hole-punch   paint   glue

Plasticine®   string   sticky tape   art straws   paper clip

◣ SCHOLASTIC
PHOTOCOPIABLE

Evaluation

You wanted your design to do these things (copy your design criteria here):	How well does your model do each of these things? (Circle a face.)
1.	 😊 🙂 🙂 ☹️
2.	 😊 🙂 🙂 ☹️
3.	 😊 🙂 🙂 ☹️

What do you think about your design overall?

_____

What new skills have you learned?

_____

WHEELS IN MOTION

Content and skills

This chapter links to Unit 2A 'Vehicles' of the QCA Scheme of Work for design and technology at Key Stage 1. In this chapter, the children will learn about wheels and axles and how to use them when making a wheeled vehicle (product) for a specific purpose.

The children will investigate a collection of toy vehicles, construction kits and pictures of wheeled vehicles and these will help them develop their own design ideas, for example a wheelbarrow to carry a specific load at a garden centre. This chapter encourages the children to think about wheels and axles. They will be investigating which parts of the vehicles move, whether all wheeled products have a moving axle, and whether all wheeled products have moving wheels. This chapter also offers opportunities to apply basic measuring skills and to draw on knowledge of forces from science.

Photograph © Dave White / iStockphoto.com

The chapter is structured as follows:
▶ Investigating and evaluating: wheeled vehicles and wheeled products.
▶ Investigating: what are different vehicles used for.
▶ Communicating ideas.
▶ Understanding axle attachments.
▶ Making the body of the vehicle.
▶ Design and make activity.
▶ Evaluating their wheeled product.

Outcome

The main outcome of this chapter will be for the children to design and make a wheeled vehicle for a specific user and purpose.

In doing this, the children will be expected to:
▶ investigate a range of wheeled vehicles and wheeled products
▶ research a range of wheeled vehicles by collecting a range of toy vehicles and pictures
▶ consider a wide variety of user needs
▶ design a wheeled vehicle (product) with a specific user in mind
▶ design, make and evaluate their wheeled vehicle (product).

Health and safety

In this chapter, the children will need to use a range of practical skills. They will be cutting card for the body of the vehicle, and using a hacksaw and a vice (or bench hook) for cutting the axles of their products. Refer to your school and local authority health and safety policies and guidelines before allowing the children to use these tools.

Links to other subjects

Science: This chapter links to science Unit 1E 'Pushes and pulls'. There are opportunities to: emphasise the difference between pushing and pulling; observe the effects of pushing and pulling on stationary objects; predict what will happen when a toy car is pushed; draw conclusions from an investigation; relate learning to everyday occurrences. The chapter also links to the science Unit 2E 'Forces and movement'. The children can suggest questions about ways in which different objects move; take measurements of distance using standard or non-standard units; decide whether their comparisons were fair.

English: There are opportunities to use skills such as questioning, describing, speaking and listening in the activities. The children will have opportunities to write about the way in which they construct their vehicle and to record results from tests. Wherever possible, the activities encourage the children to ask questions and develop an enquiring approach to their learning.

Organising the unit

All elements of the unit should be covered but the order in which they are covered can be of your own choosing. Starting points could be:

▶ investigating and evaluating different types of wheeled products

▶ investigating teacher-made examples

▶ extension from science investigations on pushes and pulls and forces (see Links section above).

Resources on the CD-ROM

The photographs on the CD-ROM are intended to supplement a collection of actual wheeled products made by yourself and the children. The images can be used for discussion purposes if models of the types of vehicles/wheeled products cannot be collected and investigated first hand. They can be looked at with different users in mind and evaluated accordingly. Photographs include: a car, police car, ambulance, fire engine, three-wheeled van, carnival float, shopping trolley, milk float and wheelbarrow.

Photocopiable pages

Photocopiable worksheets in the book and on CD-ROM include:

▶ an investigation sheet on the uses of different vehicles,

▶ worksheets for drawing labelling vehicles from different views

▶ a sheet displaying different types of axle attachments

▶ design and planning sheets to make up a process diary

▶ a sheet to encourage the children to evaluate the final product

Photocopiable sheets available on the CD-ROM only include, a set of word cards with vocabulary associated with vehicles and wheels, and labelled illustrations of equipment that might be needed (brass fasteners, sticky tape, felt-tipped pens and so on). Helpsheets are also provided with guidance on how to safely use scissors, a hacksaw, a hand drill and paper drill.

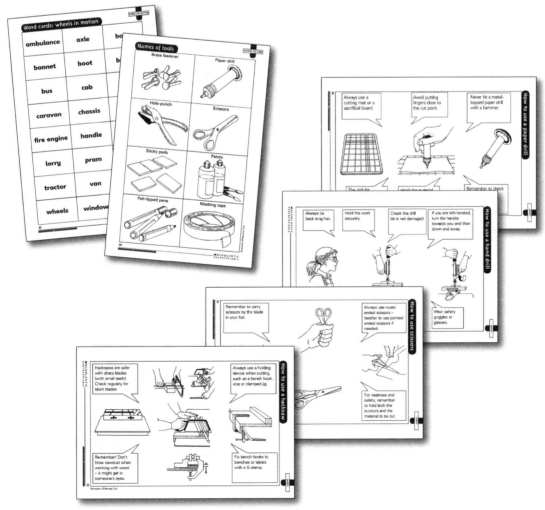

INVESTIGATING AND EVALUATING IDEAS

EXISTING WHEELED VEHICLES AND PRODUCTS

Photographs and illustrations: Fire engine, Ambulance, Police car, Post office van, Milk float, Carnival float, Car, Three-wheeled van, Pram, Shopping trolley, Wheelbarrow, Construction kit car, Car with labels

Photocopiable pages: Investigating different vehicles, Drawing a vehicle and naming the parts **PAGES 72–73**

It is important that the children are able to explore and evaluate existing wheeled vehicles. This could be a class collection of toy cars, teacher-made examples and photographs from magazines. The children could do further research on the internet, use reference books or CD-ROMs and collect pictures from home as part of a homework activity. Use the photographs on the CD-ROM to complement your own collection.

Discussing the photographs

▶ Show the photographs of vehicles and wheeled products. Have the children seen any of these vehicles and wheeled products before? Can they explain how any of them work or what they might be used for?

▶ Discuss with the children the suitability of the wheeled products for different users and different purposes, including appearance, function, comfort and safety. Can the children tell which are used in a profession (the fire engine, ambulance and police car); those that have engines; those that do not have engines (the wheelbarrow, pram and shopping trolley) and those that are intended to carry items (milk, babies and so on)? How can they tell?

▶ Look at the photograph of the 'Construction kit car', real toy vehicles and teacher-made examples in more detail and identify: which parts move, how the axles are attached, what the axle holders are made from, whether the axles move and whether the wheels move.

Activities

▶ Take photographs of a class collection of wheeled products and place these in a display with a list of their properties, for example, *fire engine – red, six wheels, hinged ladder, six seats, flashing light on top.* (Images can also be printed from the CD-ROM.)

▶ Ask the children to complete 'Investigating different vehicles' photocopiable on page 72 as part of their evaluation.

▶ Work with groups of children to choose a wheeled product and write down the five most important points in the design that has created the product.

▶ Ask the children to use the 'Drawing a vehicle and naming the parts' photocopiable on page 73 to make an observational drawing of one of the wheeled products. They should label the drawing and include: colours, decoration, logos, wheels, windows, seating, and so on. Use the photograph 'Car with labels' from the CD-ROM to demonstrate to the children what is required from them.

▶ Ask the children to investigate the different wheeled products. Encourage them to explore and identify how the vehicles move, for example, are they pushed or pulled? Investigate all the moving parts in the vehicles.

▶ Discuss with the children the different features of the vehicles. They could add to photocopiable page 73 or use a different drawing to name the moving parts of a vehicle. Explain the following terms: axle (a rod on which a wheel rotates either freely or fixed to the axle); axle holder (the component through which an axle fits); chassis (the frame on which a vehicle is built).

Photograph © Timothy Large / iStockphoto.com

WHAT ARE DIFFERENT VEHICLES USED FOR?

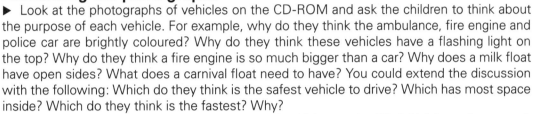

Photographs and illustrations: Fire engine, Ambulance, Police car, Post office van, Milk float, Carnival float, Car, Three-wheeled van, Pram, Shopping trolley, Wheelbarrow, Construction kit car, Car with labels

Photocopiable page: What is the vehicle used for?   PAGE 74

Discussing the photographs

▶ Look at the photographs of vehicles on the CD-ROM and ask the children to think about the purpose of each vehicle. For example, why do they think the ambulance, fire engine and police car are brightly coloured? Why do they think these vehicles have a flashing light on the top? Why do they think a fire engine is so much bigger than a car? Why does a milk float have open sides? What does a carnival float need to have? You could extend the discussion with the following: Which do they think is the safest vehicle to drive? Which has most space inside? Which do they think is the fastest? Why?

▶ Ask the children to look at the photographs of vehicles on the CD-ROM. In each case, ask who would be driving and what the purpose of the vehicle is.

▶ Using pictures from books or magazines, ask the children to describe a vehicle and the type of person who would drive it. Concentrate on the character of the person and the purpose of the vehicle that the designer would have been thinking of when he or she designed it.

Photograph © Garry Martin / iStockphoto.com

Activity

▶ Using the 'What is the vehicle used for' photocopiable on page 74 and pictures of vehicles from the CD-ROM and magazines, the children can write the names of vehicles or draw/ stick pictures of them in the chart. They can then record what each vehicle is used for, and the number of wheels.

FOCUSED PRACTICAL TASKS

COMMUNICATING IDEAS

Photocopiable page: Drawing different views   PAGE 75

Explain to the children that they will be practising their drawing and modelling skills using construction kits and reclaimed material. It is important that these skills are developed progressively through their design and technology experiences.

Discussion

▶ Discuss with the children how a car will look different, depending on the direction from which you are looking at it. Ask how they might draw a car from the front? From the side? What do they think it would look like from below?

Activities

▶ Using the 'Drawing different views' photocopiable on page 75, ask the children to draw one of the vehicles or wheeled products they have seen or studied in the photographs, from a variety of different views.

▶ Use a range of kits and other construction materials to allow the children to model their ideas, making sure that the models look right from all the different angles.

UNDERSTANDING AXLE ATTACHMENTS

Photocopiable pages: How to use a hacksaw (CD-ROM only), How to use a hand drill (CD-ROM only), Hand to use a paper drill (CD-ROM only), How to use scissors (CD-ROM only), Axle attachments **PAGE 76**

Illustration: Axle attachments

Discussing the photograph
▶ Discuss the various axle attachments shown in the illustrations on the CD-ROM. Ask the children how they will decide which one to use for their vehicle.

Activities
▶ Discuss how to use equipment safely. Demonstrate how to use a hacksaw and a vice. It is important that the correct way to stand and hold the equipment is taught beforehand, so that the children apply these rules when they are cutting materials. (Refer to the helpsheets from the CD-ROM for support.)

▶ Show the children a vehicle that has a fixed axle and moving wheels and one that has a moving axle and fixed wheels. Discuss the two types of vehicle so that they understand that wheels and axles can be assembled in two different ways: either the wheel is attached tightly to the axle and the axle is free to rotate, or the axle is fixed with the wheel free to rotate around it.

▶ Look at the illustration 'Axle attachments' from the CD-ROM and have the children try out different ways of making axle holders, for example, using cotton reels. Hand out the 'Axle attachments' photocopiable page 76 as a prompt.

▶ Ask the children to practise joining wheels and axles. They can use construction kits to model this.

MAKING THE BODY OF A VEHICLE

Photographs and illustrations: Fire engine, Ambulance, Police car, Post office van, Milk float, Carnival float, Car, Three-wheeled van, Pram, Shopping trolley, Wheelbarrow, Construction kit car, Car with labels, Hinges

Discussing the photographs
▶ Look at some of the photographs on the CD-ROM. Ask the children to observe the bodies of the vehicles and think about the different parts and shapes. Ask how they think they could build the body of the vehicle. What materials would they use and how would they fix them together?

▶ Ask the children, if they wanted to put on their vehicle, how they would add doors and windows? Some suggestions are illustrated below:

Stick one piece of carpet tape around both ends to make a hinge

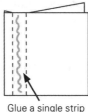

Glue a single strip inside the two pieces of card.

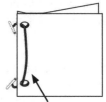

Insert a treasury tag through the punched holes.

Thread a pipe cleaner through the punched holes.

Illustration © 2008, Scholastic Ltd

Activities
▶ The children need to build up the body of the vehicle using reclaimed materials. Show them how to turn a box inside out, by taking it apart down the seam, to allow it to be painted to a high standard. The children could try out other finishing techniques, for example, computer-generated graphics or collage.

▶ Children wishing to incorporate doors in their products can practise making hinges, using the 'Hinges' illustration from the CD-ROM as a reference.

DESIGN AND MAKE ACTIVITY

DESIGN AND MAKE A WHEELED PRODUCT

Photocopiable pages: How to use a hacksaw (CD-ROM only), How to use a hand drill (CD-ROM only), Hand to use a paper drill (CD-ROM only), How to use scissors (CD-ROM only), My Design, My Plan, Word cards: Wheels in motion (CD-ROM only) **PAGES 77–78**

This activity allows the children to design and make a wheeled product or vehicle of their choosing (or you may choose to focus on a specific type). Design briefs could include:
▶ Design and make a model of a wheeled product for a particular user and purpose.
▶ Design and make a wheeled product that will move plant pots in a garden centre
▶ Design and make a vehicle to carry teddy and his/her picnic to the park.
▶ Design a trolley to keep the floor mats in the hall tidy and help move them easily.

Discussion
▶ Explain to the children that they are going to design and make a wheeled product or vehicle. They will need to use what they have learned in the focused practical tasks and investigating and evaluating activities to design and make their wheeled product or vehicle.
▶ Discuss the need to consider the purpose and user at all times when designing their wheeled product or vehicle.
▶ Display the guidance on using the tools correctly (these are in the general section of the CD-ROM) and discuss with the children of the main points of safe use.

Activities
▶ Encourage the children to use the 'My design' photocopiable on page 77 to identify what they want their vehicle or wheeled product to do: it could be a truck to be used in a garden centre to carry plant pots or a vehicle to carry teddy a certain distance when pushed or to pull teddy around the class or the playground.
▶ Encourage the children to use the 'My plan' photocopiable on page 78 to plan what they will need to make their design and to record the different stages of making. They need to consider the tools, equipment and joining methods they will use.
▶ Allow the children sufficient time to construct their model. Make sure that they are referring to their final design and planning sheet when working. Support the children in particular when they are constructing the chassis of the vehicle, which will include the axle holders, axle(s) and wheels.
▶ Use a digital camera or movie making equipment to film the children's work for reference.

EVALUATION

Photocopiable page: Evaluation **PAGE 79**

The evaluation activity is an opportunity for the children to present their vehicle to the rest of the class and to evaluate their products' success.

Discussion
▶ Display the different types of vehicles and wheeled products that the children have made. Discuss any particularly successful examples, and the variety of products they have constructed. How closely do they think the products match the original criteria?
▶ Ask individuals to present their work to the class. Encourage them to talk about any difficulties they had, and how they think the product matches their design criteria.

Activities
▶ Test the vehicles and wheeled products: *Does the vehicle move? Can the vehicle carry the teddy or the items it was designed for? Is it neatly decorated?*
▶ Ask the children to use the 'Evaluation' photocopiable on page 79, to record the evaluations against the design criteria.

Investigating different vehicles

Different vehicles		
Name of vehicle	Picture	What is it used for?
Lorry		
Pram		
Car		
Van		
Ambulance		
Caravan		
Fire engine		
Tractor		
Shopping trolly		

◣ SCHOLASTIC PHOTOCOPIABLE

Drawing a vehicle and naming the parts

Label the parts of the vehicle: body, chassis, wheels, axle, axle holders.

▲

What is the vehicle used for?

Number of wheels	Used for	Type of vehicle (name or picture, drawn or cut out from a magazine)

◀ SCHOLASTIC
PHOTOCOPIABLE

Drawing different views

▶ Choose a toy vehicle.

▶ Draw the vehicle from different views in the table below.

Front view	Side view
Top view	**Underside view**

Axle attachments

▶ Which type of axle holder will you use on your product?

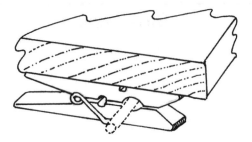

Clothes peg

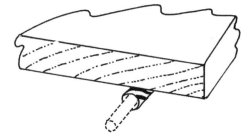

Straw

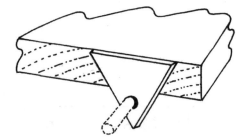

Triangle with hole

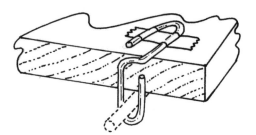

Paper clip

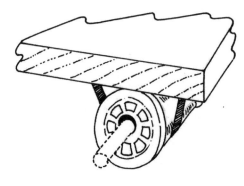

Cotton reel

■SCHOLASTIC
PHOTOCOPIABLE

My design

My vehicle will be a: _____

It will be for: _____

It will have: _____

wheel   passenger   handle   alarm

big   trailer   carry   headlights

small   people   double-decker   lock

door   driver   steering wheel

load   safety   windscreen   window

My plan

Name: _____

My design:

First I will:

Then I will:

Finally I will:

I will fix the wheels and axles with:

What else will I need?

Logos and Labels:

READY RESOURCES ▶▶ DESIGN AND TECHNOLOGY

SCHOLASTIC
PHOTOCOPIABLE

Evaluation

I designed my _____

for: _____

to: _____

It had to have:

▶ _____

▶ _____

▶ _____

The wheels on my vehicle:

☐ move very easily

☐ do not move

☐ are a bit wobbly

My vehicle is:

☐ well decorated

☐ not well decorated

Two things which are good about my vehicle are:

1. _____

2. _____

I could have made my vehicle even better by:

_____

_____

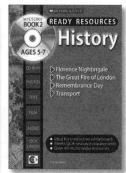
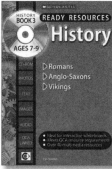

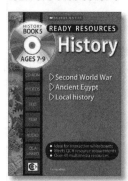

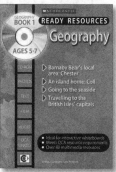
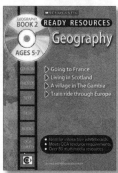
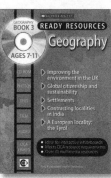
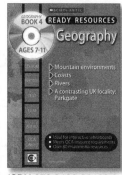
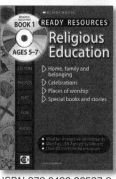
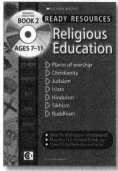